THE
History of
the Jewish People

A Story of Tradition and Change

Jonathan B. Krasner and Jonathan D. Sarna

EDITORIAL ADVISORS

Debra Beland

Rabbi Martin S. Cohen

William B. Cohen, M. A. Ed.

Professor William Cutter

Dr. Itzik Eshel

Dr. Elissa Kaplan

Rabbi Richard Hirsh

Rabbi Steven H. Rau, R. J. E.

Rabbi Yael Ridberg

Rabbi Nogah Sherman

Behrman House Publishers
www.behrmanhouse.com

Project Manager: Gila Gevirtz
Designer: Stacey May
Cartographer: Jim McMahon
Cartographic Consultant: Professor Robert M. Seltzer

The Publisher and authors gratefully acknowledge Professor Adam Rubin and Professor Ilan Troen for their generous editorial contributions to the development of *The History of the Jewish People*.

The publisher gratefully acknowledges the cooperation of the following sources of photographs and graphic images: American Jewish Archives, Cincinnati Campus, HUC- JIR: vi; American Jewish Historical Society: iv (bottom), 17, 18, 40–41, 43, 45, 46, 107; American Jewish Joint Distribution Committee: 33 (bottom), 38, 57, 58 (right), 62–63, 66, 68 (bottom), 70–71, 73, 78, 88 (bottom), 104; Bettmann/Corbis: v (top), 91, 92 (bottom), 93 (right), 94, 127; Corbis: throughout book—compass, magnifying glass, bridge span; Gila Gevirtz: v (bottom), 7, 58 (left), 114, 124, 125; Israel Consulate General Library: 88 (top); The Jewish Museum, NY/Art Resources, NY: 3, 8, 10–11, 13, 20–22, 100–101, 105 (bottom), 122–123, 129; Jewish National Fund: 27; Jerry Lampen/Reuters/Corbis: 118; Langevin Jacques/Corbis Sygma: 1 (left); Erich Lessing/Art Resources, NY: 30–31, 33 (top); Library of Congress: 14; Richard Lobell: 98; Richard T. Nowitz/Corbis: 1 (right); Jeremy Poisson: 131; Eric Pollitzer: 72; Arnold Pronto/ The Helen Suzman Foundation: 106; Alon Reininger: 85; Reuters/Corbis: 110–111, 120, 117; Edward Serotta: 112; Snark/Art Resources, NY: 65; State of Israel Government Press Office: 28 (top); Robert F. Wagner Labor Archives: 42; World Wide Photos: 56; Yad Vashem: 68 (top), 75, 77, 82; YIVO Institute of Jewish Research Archives, NY: 33 (middle), 34, 92 (top), 93 (left), 103; Zionist Archives and Library: 28 (bottom), 52– 53, 54, 60; American Jewish Historical Society, Gila Gevirtz, Israel Consulate General Library, The Jewish Museum, NY/Art Resources, NY, Jewish National Fund, Jeremy Poisson, Eric Pollitzer, YIVO Institute of Jewish Research Archives, NY: cover

To Sylvia C. Ettenberg, a visionary who raised the bar

— J.B.K. and J.D.S.

CONTENTS

Why Be Jewish?		vi
1.	East European Jewry, 1881–1914	2
2.	The Great Migration	10
3.	Jewish Nationalism and Zionism	20
4.	World War I	30
5.	At Home in the U.S., 1920–1940	40
6.	The British Mandate	52
7.	Europe Between the Wars	62

8. The Holocaust   70

9. The Birth of the Modern State of Israel   80

10. "Making It" in America, 1945–1965   90

11. The Diaspora Consolidates   100

12. Israel in Our Time   110

13. American Jewry Today   122

Glossary   132

Index   135

Why Be Jewish?

Every year at the Passover seder we read the story of how our people were delivered from slavery in Pharaoh's Egypt. We eat bitter herbs to remind us of the pain we suffered and recline in our chairs, thankful that we are now free.

Passover's message of hope and freedom has inspired every generation since the Exodus. In the year 70, when the Land of Israel was conquered by the Romans, our people were dispersed to foreign lands. In time, we built Jewish communities in places as distant as Babylonia, Spain, Germany, and France. When new Pharaohs sought to enslave or destroy us, we traveled on and built new communities.

The first Jewish community in North America was founded in 1654 by twenty-three settlers. The Jews grew in numbers and wealth, fought in the American Revolution, and were granted full rights along with non-Jewish citizens. This meant that they could vote, run for public office, own land, and honor their religion without government interference.

By the end of the nineteenth century, this freedom—often called emancipation—spread throughout Western Europe. In Russia and Poland, where the majority of the world's Jews lived, emancipation came only in the early twentieth century.

The history of the Jewish people includes the history of many peoples and many lands.

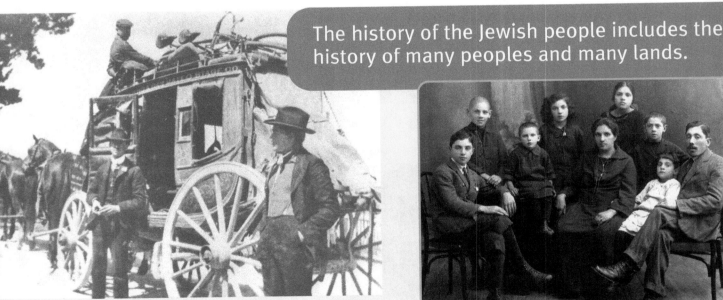

The Levy brothers were born in Western Europe. In the 1870's, they immigrated to the United States where they developed a range of businesses including a stagecoach line.

The Bub family left Latvia in about 1927, in search of freedom and economic opportunity. Today, they have more than one hundred and fifty descendants living in Israel, South Africa, Australia, the United Kingdom, the United States, and Canada.

Emancipation meant that Jews could become full-fledged citizens. As discrimination against them decreased, Jews were able to live where they wanted, earn their living as they chose, and participate in government. But, in both Europe and the United States, emancipation proved to be a double-edged sword. On the one hand, it brought great benefits, such as expanded educational, social, and economic possibilities. On the other hand, it carried the risk that Jews might decide to abandon their religious beliefs and practices. For the first time in history, Jews could not only choose *how* to live as Jews, but could also choose *not* to live as Jews.

As you read *The History of the Jewish People*, you will discover the effect that emancipation had on Jewish communities around the world; the ways emancipation changed the religious and social practices of Jews; and the ways emancipation changed Judaism itself.

In addition, you will see how your life compares with the lives of those who came before you and how their decisions affect your life. Most especially, you will consider why Jews choose to remain Jewish. Having gained the freedom to be like all other citizens in every aspect of our lives, why do so many of us still maintain our Jewish identities?

Due to conflict between the Jews and Muslims of Yemen, the majority of Jews immigrated to Israel between 1949 and 1950. Today, only small numbers of Jews live in Yemen, like this family from Raydah.

These Israeli children are performing a dance for Purim in Jerusalem. In Israel, Purim is not only a *religious* holiday, it is also a *national* holiday.

Chapter 1

East European Jewry, 1881–1914

A Time of Turmoil and Transformation

investigate

- How did the pogroms of 1881 and 1882 change the lives of Russian Jews?

- What were the three major responses of the Jewish community?

- How did those responses help shape the Jewish world of today?

Key Words and Places

Pale of Settlement	Palestine
Pogroms	Socialism
The Protocols of the Elders of Zion	Bund

The BIG Picture

In every life, certain events stand out as turning points: the day one celebrates becoming a bar or bat mitzvah, marries, has a child, or suffers a great loss, like the death of a loved one. Whether the event is cause for celebration or sadness, somehow one never feels quite the same again.

So it is in the life of a people. Jewish history has key turning points, including the Maccabees' revolt in 167 BCE, the destruction of the Second Temple in 70 CE, and the expulsion of the Jews from Spain in 1492. For better or worse, each turning point separated all that had come before from everything that happened after.

A great wave of antisemitic riots in 1881 and 1882 created just such a turning point. These attacks shook the foundations of Russian Jewry—which, at about five million, was the largest population of Jews in the world at that time. The pogroms made it clear to the Jews that they had to take matters into their own hands.

1855

Alexander II becomes czar of Russia, lifts many anti-Jewish restrictions

1881

Czar Alexander II assassinated; Alexander III becomes czar; issues anti-Jewish laws

1882

First settlement in Palestine established by ten Russian Jews

Hope for Greater Opportunities

When Alexander II became the czar of Russia in 1855, Russian Jews looked on with hope as they gained new freedom. Before Alexander, anti-Jewish prejudice had influenced Russian leaders to insist that all Jews live in the **Pale of Settlement,** the land that included much of present-day Lithuania, Poland, Belarus, Ukraine, and Moldova, so that the Jewish population would not spread throughout the Russian Empire. Now, under Czar Alexander II, restrictions on Jewish settlement were loosened. In addition, Jewish children no longer were forced to join the Russian army.

While many Jews maintained their traditional religious lifestyle, others were influenced by the ideas of the *Haskalah*, the Jewish Enlightenment, which emphasized secular learning and integration into the larger society. They began to attend government-sponsored schools and universities, studying Russian and other secular subjects. Eager to join the middle class, many looked forward to leaving their small towns and villages in search of greater opportunities in cities.

1896	1897	1900	1903	1905
World History: First modern Olympic Games held in Athens, Greece	General Jewish Workers Union (Bund) formed; has 40,000 members by 1906	By this date, nearly half of all Jews in Eastern Europe live in cities	Antisemitic *Protocols of the Elders of Zion* first printed in Russia	More than 1,000 Jews murdered in large wave of antisemitic riots in Russia

The Tides of Fortune Turn

But in March 1881, Czar Alexander II was assassinated by anti-czarist revolutionaries and Jewish hopes for a better life ended. Economic problems in the years before the czar's death had created resentment among the Russian people. Now they wanted a scapegoat, someone to blame. Anti-Jewish propaganda blamed the Jews for the czar's assassination, even though only one of the revolutionaries who carried out the assassination was Jewish. Throughout the spring and summer of 1881 the Russian government idly stood by as a wave of massacres, or **pogroms,** violently swept through parts of the Pale.

Motivated by religious extremism, Russia's new czar, Alexander III, hated the Jews and wanted to isolate them from the rest of society. He issued laws that imposed limits on where Jews could live, how many could attend high schools and universities, and what jobs they could hold. As a senior member of the government is said to have admitted, the policies were designed so that "one-third [of the Jews] will die out, one-third will leave the country, and one-third will be completely absorbed into the surrounding population."

The anti-Jewish policies continued under Czar Nicholas II and new waves of pogroms broke out after a failed anti-czarist revolution in 1905. Six hundred and sixty communities were attacked and over one thousand Jews were murdered. Determined to fight back against their attackers, Jews in some cities organized self-defense groups.

The Protocols of the Elders of Zion

The Russian secret police produced a false document called *The Protocols of the Elders of Zion*. It claimed to provide a record of secret meetings at which Jewish leaders made plans to overthrow governments and seize world power.

First printed in a Russian newspaper in 1903, the *Protocols* were widely translated and circulated by antisemitic groups in Europe and the United States. Although the London *Times* proved in 1921 that the *Protocols* was a forgery, some continued to use it to justify antisemitic actions. It is still distributed by antisemitic groups today, including in parts of the Muslim world.

Hundreds of Jews were killed or maimed in pogroms, and much of the property Jews owned was destroyed.

Unstable economic conditions fueled Russian antisemitism. Fears that Russia was falling behind the West prompted the government to push for modernization and industrialization. New factories replaced traditional peasant industries. For example, factory-made clothes replaced handmade clothes and railroads replaced the traditional horse and buggy. At the same time, modern agricultural methods increased harvests so that fewer farmers were needed. Many farmers could no longer make a living. The government, church, and newspapers encouraged the population to redirect their anxiety about these economic changes into antisemitic actions, such as pogroms.

Peddlers suffered because trains brought goods to distant places faster than peddlers could travel, and, in any case, fewer people in small villages could afford the goods.

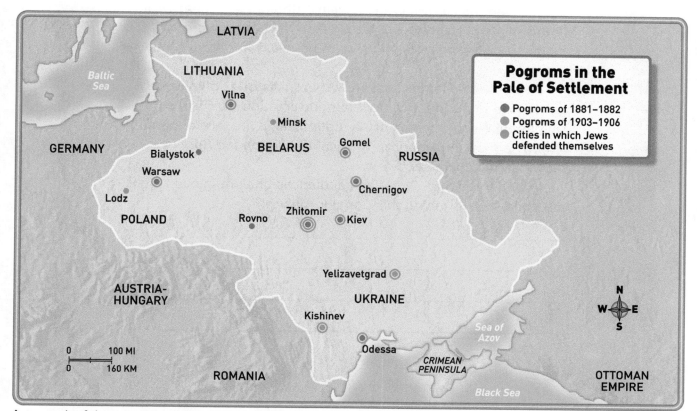

As a result of the pogroms, many Jews emigrated from the Pale of Settlement—the majority to the United States, Western Europe, and Palestine.

Famous FIGURES

Sholom Aleichem

Sholom Aleichem (holding book) with his family

Despite worsening conditions, the late 1800's and early 1900's were decades of Jewish cultural renewal in Eastern Europe. Yiddish stories, theater, and popular music found eager audiences.

Many of the most famous Yiddish authors lived at this time. Sholom Aleichem (1859–1916) was the pen name of Solomon Rabinovitz. Considered by many to be the greatest Yiddish humorist, he is often called the "Jewish Mark Twain." Sholom Aleichem wrote in Russian and Hebrew, but his greatest successes were in Yiddish—including forty volumes of novels, short stories, and plays.

Sholom Aleichem is best known for his stories of everyday Jewish life in Russia. His most famous creation was Tevye the Dairyman, who remained firmly optimistic in the face of hardship. The modern American musical *Fiddler on the Roof* is based on the character Tevye.

Why do you think American audiences of all religious beliefs are interested in seeing this popular musical?

_____

_____

_____

_____

Economic changes were also affecting many Jews. The growth of railroads and deterioration of Russia's peasant-based economy ruined the livelihoods of Jewish merchants, peddlers, artisans, and innkeepers whose services were no longer needed. By the 1880's Jewish poverty was common in parts of Eastern Europe.

Socialism and the Bund

Among those most disappointed by events in Russia were the *Maskilim*, the Jewish intellectuals and professionals who had tried to integrate into Russian society. They, too, now saw little hope that czarist Russia would ever grant Jews the full rights of citizens.

Some Jews became convinced that they would have to gain their own freedom. To do this, they believed, Jews had to revive Hebrew as their national language, return to their native Land of Israel, and rebuild the Jewish nation. During this period, the first groups of Russian immigrants began their journey to **Palestine,** which is what the Land of Israel was called then.

But the majority of Jews were determined to remain in Russia and improve their lives there. Many city dwellers joined with other Russians who were striving to better the conditions of working people. They formed trade unions and went on strike to help achieve their goals. The Jewish trade unions and intellectual groups combined the economic and political ideals of **Socialism**—the belief that society should be based on cooperation rather than competition—with Jewish values of social justice.

In 1897 the local organizations united to form a single Socialist party, the General Jewish

Jaffa was a port city in ancient Israel. This detail of a memorial in modern Jaffa honors the diverse groups that restored the city's Jewish community as early as the beginning of the nineteenth century.

Workers Union, popularly known as the **Bund**. Bund-led strikes won improved working conditions. And when a new wave of pogroms broke out between 1903 and 1906, the Bund took the lead in organizing Jews into local self-defense groups. It fired the imaginations of tens of thousands of Jewish youths with its vision of a Russia free from czars. By 1906 the Bund boasted over 40,000 members, a remarkable number given that the major Russian Socialist party had only 150,000 members.

The Great Debate:
Hebrew versus Yiddish Culture

Hebrew culture as well as Yiddish culture thrived at the beginning of the twentieth century. Supporters of Hebrew culture were determined to revive the Jewish holy language as a living language. The most famous supporter was Ḥayyim Naḥman Bialik, whose poetry expressed not only the anguish, despair, and shame that Jews felt in the face of the pogroms, but also celebrated the beauty of Russian Jewish life.

Bialik began writing in Yiddish, but soon abandoned it for Hebrew. While he and other writers used both languages, as well as Polish and Russian to reach different audiences, the conflict between Yiddishists and Hebraists was often fierce. In choosing one language over the other, a writer made the political statement: "I support the Bund" or "I support the return to Palestine."

In some cases, the conflict between Yiddishists and Hebraists threatened to tear apart families. Solomon Rabinovitz chose to write under the pen name Sholom Aleichem because, as a Yiddish writer, he was afraid of angering his father who supported the return to Palestine. The meaning of his pen name, "Peace be with you," was not simply a clever play on a popular Jewish greeting, but also a plea for tolerance.

Seeking New Homes

Meanwhile, many Jews were on the move, flocking to cities like Warsaw, Vilna, Vienna, and Budapest. By 1900 almost half the Jewish population of Eastern Europe lived in cities. The Jewish population of Warsaw grew from 3,500 to 220,000, making Jews one-third of the city's population. Russia's five million Jews represented only 4 percent of the population, yet Jews made up a majority of the city dwellers in the Pale of Settlement.

Even greater numbers of Jews left Eastern Europe and Russia altogether. Some moved to Western Europe. A few thousand settled in Palestine, and thousands more went to South Africa, Argentina, and Canada. But the great majority went to the United States. Between 1881 and 1914, more than two million East European Jews immigrated to the United States.

The unstable economic and social conditions drove many Jews to seek new opportunities outside of Russia. How would you describe the scene and mood portrayed in this 1910 painting, *After the Pogrom?*

Believing that the best way to ensure their emancipation, or freedom from oppression, was to take matters into their own hands, the Jews of Russia came up with diverse solutions. The three most popular solutions were:

- Remain in Russia and create a more just society by combining Jewish values of social justice with the ideals of Socialism.
- Return to the Land of Israel and rebuild the Jewish nation.
- Move to the United States, which offered greater religious and economic freedom.

1. Imagine that you were living in Russia in the late nineteenth century. Which of the three choices would you make? Why?

_____

_____

_____

2. Explain how your choice could help you maintain and strengthen your Jewish identity.

_____

_____

3. Describe one challenge you face in maintaining your Jewish identity in today's world and one solution to the challenge.

_____

_____

_____

Chapter 2 The Great Migration
New Challenges to Jewish Tradition

investigate

- What challenges did the Russian Jews find in America?
- What contributions did they make?
- How did they express their Jewish identities?
- In what ways can they be role models for us today?

Key Words and Places

Ellis Island

Tenement Houses

Sweatshops

Labor Movement

Sephardic Jews

The BIG Picture

Abraham Cahan was a wanted man.

The year was 1881, and Abraham Cahan actively opposed the czar's regime. This twenty-one-year-old son of a Hebrew teacher yearned for greater freedom and social equality. He had just graduated from the Vilna Teachers' Institute when, suddenly, the assassination of Czar Alexander II brought a crackdown on anyone suspected of anti-czarist activities. With the secret police on his heels, Cahan sailed for America in 1882.

Abraham Cahan was one of more than two million Jews from Russia and Eastern Europe to make this journey between 1881 and 1914. These courageous and accomplished immigrants helped create the vibrant American Jewish communities we know today.

1885

Jewish Theological Seminary of America founded; headed by Rabbi Sabato Morais

1892

Ellis Island immigration center opens in New York Harbor

1893

Lillian Wald founds Visiting Nurse Service and Henry Street Settlement

Difficult Decisions

Leaving home is never easy. For Abraham Cahan, it meant leaving friends, relatives, and even his beloved parents. But, like many others, he knew that there were too many mouths to feed, not enough money for food, and little hope that social and economic conditions would soon improve. Young Jewish males in Russia also faced the threat of being forced to enlist in the czar's army. Conditions in the army were harsh and discrimination against Jews was common. Finally, there were the brutal waves of pogroms, especially in 1880–1881, 1903, and 1905.

If some factors *pushed* Jews away from Russia and Eastern Europe, others *pulled* them toward the United States. Railroads and steamships made long journeys easier, safer, and cheaper than ever before. In addition, European Jews were hearing a lot about the freedom and opportunities in the United States.

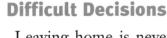

1908

World History:
Henry Ford
introduces Model T,
first car to be
mass-produced

1909

Clara Lemlich helps
lead strike of
women working in
clothing industry

1911

Fire at the
Triangle
Shirtwaist factory
in New York City

1914

U.S. Jewish population
reaches 3 million; largest
Jewish community in
world outside of Russia

Push Factors Driving Jews Away from Russia and Eastern Europe

◎ Poverty

◎ Pogroms

◎ Fear of being forced to serve in the military

◎ Overpopulation

Pull Factors Driving Jews Toward the United States

◎ Economic opportunities in the United States

◎ Safety

◎ Freedom

◎ Encouragement of friends and relatives who had settled in the United States

You Are There

Eastern Europe

Going to America?

Imagine you are living in Eastern Europe in the early 1900's. Will you leave everything behind and make the trip to America? In addition to economic and social concerns, you have religious concerns. You've heard that America is an "unkosher land," a place where observing Shabbat and keeping kosher are almost impossible. In fact, some famous European rabbis warn against settling in America. They insist that it is better to be poor and religiously observant in Europe than to be rich and spiritually lost in America. In contrast, friends and relatives have told you that freedom makes all things possible and that in America immigrants can make religious choices for themselves.

List two reasons why you would move to America and two reasons why you would stay in Eastern Europe.

Move to America _____

_____

Stay in Eastern Europe _____

_____

This Rosh Hashanah greeting card from the early twentieth century portrays Jewish immigrants arriving in the United States.

The Challenges of Making a New Home

Even after making the decision to leave home, immigrants faced great challenges in leaving the country. Like many Russian Jews, Abraham Cahan was not allowed to leave Russia legally.

After sneaking across the border, he made his way to the port city of Hamburg, Germany. From there he went by boat to England, then sailed from Liverpool on the ship *British Queen* for the United States. Like most immigrants, Cahan could only afford a steerage ticket, which meant living in foul-smelling cabins belowdecks for the two-week trip across the Atlantic.

There were more challenges once Jewish immigrants set foot on dry land and passed through the **Ellis Island** immigration center. The first was finding a place to live. Many moved into Jewish urban, or city, neighborhoods, near relatives or people from their old hometowns. The Jewish populations of New York City, Chicago, Boston, Philadelphia, Baltimore, and Cleveland shot upward.

Manhattan's Lower East Side attracted more Jewish immigrants than any other neighborhood. It quickly became one of the most densely populated spots on earth. In the

After disembarking from their ships at Ellis Island, new immigrants waited in large holding pens to be processed by immigration officials. They received quick medical exams and were asked a series of questions about where they came from, where they were going, and what they intended to do in the United States. If their health or responses were not considered acceptable, they were sent back to Europe.

Disease and fire were constant dangers in the cramped tenements.

Lower East Side, immigrants crammed into five- and six-story brick buildings, often called **tenement houses** or simply tenements. Families of eight or more frequently shared tiny, sometimes windowless, tenement apartments.

The second challenge for immigrants was finding work. Some became peddlers, traveling great distances or going door-to-door to sell their goods. Others found jobs in the

Jews and the Labor Movement

With thousands of Jews working in low-paying and often dangerous jobs, it is no surprise that Jews were among the leaders of the U.S. labor movement—the organized effort to improve working conditions—in the late 1800's. In 1866, Samuel Gompers, a Jewish immigrant from England, became the first president of the American Federation of Labor (AFL). The original membership of the AFL was estimated at about 140,000 workers who came from twenty-five different national workers' unions.

By the time labor leader Clara Lemlich was nineteen, she had been arrested seventeen times for organizing sweatshop workers into unions. On November 22, 1909, at a huge meeting of workers in New York's shirtwaist factories, manufacturers of women's clothing, the fearless Lemlich rose and shouted, "I have listened to all the speakers. I would not have further patience for talk.... I move that we go on a general strike!"

Lemlich and others continued pushing for change, but it was a disaster at New York's Triangle Shirtwaist Company that brought national attention to workers' demands. On March 25, 1911, a fire started on the eighth floor of the factory, trapping workers who were locked inside and killing 146 people, most of them young Jewish and Italian women. The public was horrified, and labor unions finally began winning improvements in working conditions.

Many Jewish immigrants, like these striking shirt-waist-makers, supported their families by working long hours in unsafe factories.

fast-growing garment industry, or clothing trade, which became New York City's biggest industry in the early 1900's. More than 80 percent of New York's clothing factories were owned by Jews and employed Jews. Thousands worked twelve- and fourteen-hour workdays in hot, cramped workshops known as **sweatshops.**

The arrival of hundreds of thousands of Jewish immigrants in a short period of time sometimes led to tension between the recent and the more established Jewish immigrants. Some, who had been in the country for a generation or more, worried that the newer immigrants who wore Old World clothing and spoke Yiddish would become an embarrassment to them. Far more often, however, American Jews reached out to help the new arrivals adjust, providing English classes, free libraries, and the chance to learn practical job skills.

New World Challenges to Ancient Traditions

Along with newfound freedom and opportunity, East European Jewish immigrants also faced new challenges: *What to do when there is a conflict between Jewish law and American ways of life?* Back in the shtetls, for example, Shabbat was observed as a traditional day of rest by many Jews. In America, Saturday was a workday. Many factories posted signs that read: "If you don't come in on Saturday, don't bother coming in on Monday." Jews faced the choice between losing their job or violating Shabbat.

In Eastern Europe, the Jews had asked, "What must I do to remain safe from people who harm me?" In the United States they asked, "What Jewish traditions will stand in the way of my succeeding in America?"

Write one question you have about the importance or challenge of living as a Jew in America.

_____

_____

Lillian Wald

Lillian Wald (1867–1940) was born into a wealthy Jewish family in Cincinnati, Ohio. Although her wealth permitted her to choose a life of luxury, Wald became a nurse, dedicating herself to the relief of human pain and suffering.

In 1893, Wald founded the Visiting Nurse Service and the Henry Street Settlement. These institutions provided important services to immigrants and the poor—Jewish and non-Jewish alike—including home health care and instruction in hygiene, parenting, English, and the arts. In addition, Wald fought for laws to protect the rights of women and children and was an active member of the Women's Peace Party.

Lillian Wald

Not everyone dedicated to helping others is famous. Describe someone you know personally who is dedicated to helping others. Describe an action that shows the person's commitment. If you like, include the person's name and profession or relationship to you.

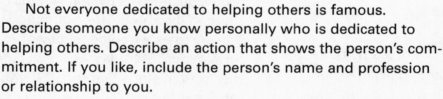

This map appeared in John Foster Carr's *Guide to the United States for the Jewish Immigrant* in 1916. The names of states and their capitals and major cities are listed in English and transliterated using Yiddish letters.

Can you find the Yiddish transliteration of "Canada"?

Like the Russian Jews, American Jews worked to improve their own lives and the lives of other Jews in their communities. Jewish communities in both countries had charities that helped the needy.

Jews in Russia

◎ Formed Jewish trade unions and went on strike to improve working conditions

◎ Organized local Jewish self-defense groups in response to pogroms

Jews in America

◎ Helped organize labor unions to improve working conditions

◎ Aided Jewish immigrants through tzedakah and education to help newcomers integrate into American society and earn a living

The Changing Map of World Jewry

More than two and a half million Jews settled in new countries between 1881 and 1914. Significant communities of East European immigrants developed in Western Europe, Canada, Argentina, South Africa, and even far-off Australia, as well as the Land of Israel.

But by far the largest number—eight out of ten—ended up in the United States, changing the map of world Jewry forever. New York City suddenly was home to the largest Jewish community in the world. In fact, it had the largest Jewish community in the history of the world to that time. By World War I, the United States

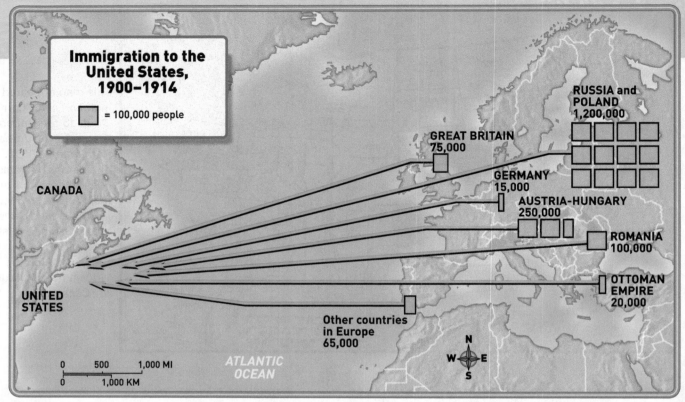

Immigration to the United States, 1900–1914

☐ = 100,000 people

RUSSIA and POLAND
1,200,000

GREAT BRITAIN
75,000

GERMANY
15,000

AUSTRIA-HUNGARY
250,000

ROMANIA
100,000

OTTOMAN EMPIRE
20,000

CANADA

UNITED STATES

Other countries in Europe
65,000

ATLANTIC OCEAN

0   500   1,000 MI
0   1,000 KM

Escaping persecution and poverty, wave after wave of Jews, particularly from Eastern Europe, immigrated to the United States between 1900 and 1914.

was home to about three million Jews, more than anywhere else except the Russian Empire, where almost seven million Jews still lived.

Between fifty and sixty thousand **Sephardic Jews**—Jews of Spanish origin—from Turkey, Greece, and the Middle East also settled in the United States during these years. Some of them spoke Arabic and others Greek, but most spoke Ladino, a language based on Spanish and Hebrew. New York City, where most of the Sephardic Jews settled, became the most important Sephardic community outside of the Ottoman Empire. A large Sephardic community also developed in Seattle, Washington.

By World War I, the great migration had brought Jews to six continents. For most, it led to a better life. Abraham Cahan, for example, became editor of the leading Yiddish newspaper in the United States, the *Forward*.

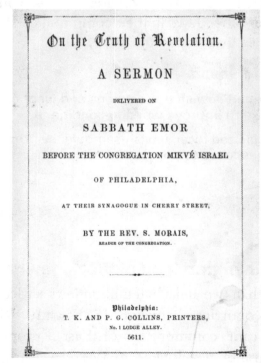

On the Truth of Revelation.

A SERMON

DELIVERED ON

SABBATH EMOR

BEFORE THE CONGREGATION MIKVÉ ISRAEL

OF PHILADELPHIA,

AT THEIR SYNAGOGUE IN CHERRY STREET,

BY THE REV. S. MORAIS,
READER OF THE CONGREGATION.

Philadelphia:
T. K. AND P. G. COLLINS, PRINTERS,
No. 1 LODGE ALLEY.
5611.

Rabbi Sabato Morais (1823–1897) was a Sephardic poet, historian, and educator, and one of the founders of the Jewish Theological Seminary in New York.

then & NOW

Jewish immigrants found themselves torn between two competing attractions. On the one hand, they sought to *adapt* to their new surroundings. They studied English, wore American clothes, and participated in civic life. They sent their children to public schools, absorbed local culture and sports, and learned how to be good citizens. On the other hand, they also wanted to *retain* their Jewish identities. They usually lived near other Jews, observed Jewish holidays, kept kosher, and, if East European, spoke Yiddish among themselves. Their goal was to become part of their new land yet maintain their Jewish way of life.

1. List two things you do that reflect your identity as an American citizen.

   A. _____

   B. _____

2. List two things you do that reflect your Jewish identity.

   A. _____

   B. _____

3. Describe one way in which maintaining your Jewish identity can help you be a better American.

   _____

   _____

4. Describe a situation in which living as a Jew might create a challenge for you. What could you do to overcome the challenge?

   _____

   _____

   _____

3 Jewish Nationalism and Zionism
Imagining a Modern Jewish State

investigate

- Why did the idea of creating a modern Jewish state develop?

- How did the success or failure of emancipation in a country affect the Jews' support of such a state?

- What were the different visions of what the Jewish state should be?

- How does the existence of Israel influence our Jewish identities today?

Key Words and Places

Ashkenazic Jews

Diaspora

Nationalism

Ḥovevei Tzion

Aliyah

First Aliyah

Zionism

First Zionist Congress

World Zionist Organization (WZO)

Hatikvah

Uganda Plan

Second Aliyah

Yishuv

Jewish National Fund (JNF)

The BIG Picture

The Jewish longing for the Land of Israel is as old as the Diaspora—the dispersion of the Jews to countries outside of Israel. In the Bible we read of the Jewish exiles in Babylon who wept for Zion—Jerusalem—after the destruction of the Holy Temple in 586 BCE. The Book of Psalms expresses their grief in these words: "If I forget you, O Jerusalem, let my right hand wither; let my tongue stick to the roof of my mouth..."

After the Second Temple was destroyed in 70 CE, Jews prayed for the rebuilding of Zion. Century after century, we repeated such prayers at our Passover seders, on the fast of Tisha B'Av, which commemorates the Temple's destruction, and three times a day during the Amidah. Most Jews understood these prayers as an appeal for the speedy coming of the Messiah. But in the late 1800's, a small group of passionate Jews committed their lives to turning the dream of a return to Zion into a reality.

1882

First Aliyah begins; brings first wave of Jews to Palestine in response to Zionism

1884

Students and workers found *Ḥovevei Tzion* to work for establishment of Jewish state

1895

French authorities unjustly convict Alfred Dreyfus, a French Jew, of spying

1897

Herzl holds First Zionist Congress in Basel, Switzerland

Palestine Before 1880

For almost two thousand years after the fall of Jerusalem in 70 CE, Palestine was controlled by a series of rulers from different countries and empires. Conditions were often difficult for the Jews of Palestine, but their fortunes improved in the early sixteenth century when the Ottoman Turks gained control. Although Jews had second-class status under Muslim law, the Turks were tolerant rulers. Palestine became a refuge for many Jews who had been forced out of Spain at the end of the fifteenth century.

Legal reforms in the 1840's and 1850's brought greater equality for the Jews and resulted in increased Jewish immigration. By 1880 there were about twenty thousand Jews in Palestine, making up about 5 percent of the population. The majority of the population was Muslim and Christian Arab. Most of the Jews were Sephardic Jews. But many of the newer arrivals were **Ashkenazic Jews,** Jews of German origin who came from Eastern Europe. Almost all the Jews lived in cities, settling in Safed, Tiberias, Hebron, and Jerusalem, considered particularly holy towns according to Jewish tradition. Most Jews lived in poverty, surviving on charity from the **Diaspora,** Jewish communities outside the Land of Israel.

1901
Jewish National Fund founded

1903
World History: Wright Brothers make world's first successful airplane flight

1905
Second Aliyah begins; brings new wave of Jewish immigration to Palestine

1909
Jewish settlers begin construction of city that will become Tel Aviv

Jews praying at the Western Wall, a supporting wall of the ancient Temple in Jerusalem, in about 1880.

The Dream of Jewish Nationalism

A wave of **nationalism**—pride in one's nation— swept across Europe in the 1800's. Nationalists argued that every nation—a people who shared a common language, history, and land—had a right to govern itself in its own homeland.

The influence of nationalism inspired a few dreamers to become *Jewish* nationalists. With the rise in antisemitism, more Jews were drawn to the idea of Jewish nationalism. Leon Pinsker, a Jewish doctor and author, believed that self-protection required that the Jews free themselves and live in a country of their own. Jews, Pinsker wrote, "are everywhere as *guests*, and nowhere *at home*." Many of his followers were young students and workers in Russia, Austria-Hungary, and Romania. Organizing into small clubs called **Ḥovevei Tzion,** or Lovers of Zion, they held their first convention in 1884 and elected Pinsker as their president.

The First Aliyah

Pinsker cared that a Jewish state be created, but not *where* it was created. In contrast, most of his followers believed that Jewish nationalism would be meaningless unless its goal was a return to the Land of Israel. *Ḥovevei Tzion* began raising money, sponsoring classes in Jewish history and Hebrew, and organizing self-defense groups, called Maccabee clubs. Their goal: *aliyah,* "going up" to and settling in the Land of Israel.

The first group began arriving in Palestine in the summer of 1882. And so began what is known as the **First Aliyah,** the first wave of Jews who moved to Palestine in response to the movement to create a modern Jewish state. The First Aliyah took place from 1882 to 1903. Some of the new immigrants became artisans, shopkeepers, and hired farmhands. Others were poorly prepared to earn a living in Palestine and returned to Europe or moved to North America.

The existing Jewish community was very different from the nationalists of the First Aliyah. Unlike the new arrivals, their connection to the Land of Israel was based on religious ties and they were generally content to wait for the Messiah rather than build up the land.

The hardiest among the new settlers soon established farming colonies. The first was named Rishon L'tziyon. By 1905 there were about twenty such settlements. Today, many have become thriving towns and cities. But in the early years most struggled to survive. Threatened by malaria, poverty, and a lack of farming experience, the early Jewish colonists often lived on the edge of ruin.

Theodor Herzl

Meanwhile, events in Europe gave new life to **Zionism,** the movement to create a modern

פוט. י. בן-דוב תלמיד „בצלאל" ירושלם.
המרכז „בראשון לציון".
Centrum i Rischon-le-Zion.
№ 121 חברת „לבונן"

The name Rishon L'tziyon was inspired by this biblical reference to the coming of the Messiah: "Behold, here they are, the first to bring the news of the Messiah to Zion—*rishon l'tziyon*" (Isaiah 41:27). Why do you think the settlers chose that name?

Jewish state. In 1895, Theodor Herzl, a young Austrian-Jewish journalist, was in Paris when Colonel Alfred Dreyfus, a French Jew, was unjustly convicted of spying. On January 6, 1895, Herzl witnessed Dreyfus's humiliation as he was publicly stripped of his rank. Herzl listened in horror as the crowd of twenty thousand shouted, "Death to the traitor! Death to the Jews!"

Responding to this injustice, Herzl published a short book called *The Jewish State.* His message: emancipation had been a failure for the Jews; they still were not safe in Europe. Only a massive movement from Europe to their own land would end antisemitism.

Herzl's ideas received an icy reception from leading Jews in the West. The Jews of Western Europe were full citizens and most were eager to demonstrate their patriotism to the nations in which they lived. But the Jews in Eastern Europe and Russia were not yet emancipated. Thus Herzl's ideas sparked great excitement among them.

On August 29, 1897, Herzl held the **First Zionist Congress** in Basel, Switzerland. More than two hundred delegates from Jewish communities in sixteen different countries elected Herzl as their leader and adopted his plan. They founded the **World Zionist Organization (WZO)** and made **Hatikvah,** meaning "The Hope," the hymn of the Zionist movement.

So as not to offend the Turks, the Congress avoided using the term "state" in describing Zionism's goals. But in his diary Herzl declared: "In Basel, I created the Jewish State."

To Be or Not to Be a Jewish State

For the next few years, Herzl traveled tirelessly from capital to capital, meeting with leaders of the great powers, working to win support for the idea of a homeland for the Jews. While he hoped it would be in Palestine, his first concern was to achieve the political goal of establishing a state. Herzl wanted a state for the Jews, not necessarily a "Jewish" state. He had given a lot of thought to a future state's form of government and economy, but he was not especially concerned about the content of its Jewish culture. Herzl assumed, for example, that its official language would be German, not Hebrew.

So, when Herzl determined that the Ottoman rulers had no intention of parting with Palestine, he was open to considering other options. One such option was the British offer of land in East Africa. That option became known as the **Uganda Plan.**

Theodor Herzl

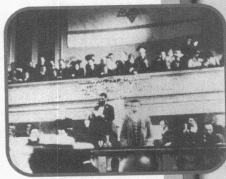

Theodor Herzl (standing left of center) addressing the First Zionist Congress

Theodor Herzl (1860–1904) was an unlikely father of Zionism. Born into a middle-class family in Budapest, Herzl was a great admirer of German culture and spent most of his early life trying to fit into European high society. While studying at the University of Vienna, he joined a respected fraternity with few Jewish members.

Despite Herzl's best hopes, the anti-semitism of his fraternity brothers forced him to quit the group in disgust. He suffered another painful blow when Vienna elected an openly antisemitic mayor. But it was the antisemitism in France, home of the ideals of "Liberty, Equality, and Brotherhood," that troubled Herzl most.

At first, antisemitism made Herzl ashamed of his Jewish identity. As late as 1893, he proposed the idea of a mass conversion of Jews to Catholicism. But Herzl changed his mind less than six months after Dreyfus was sent to Devil's Island prison. By then, he had concluded that founding a Jewish state was the only solution for the Jews of Europe.

Herzl's Zionist slogan was: "If you will it, it is no dream." What do you think that means?

_____

_____

Describe a dream that Jews might have today? What could you do to help that dream come true?

_____

_____

You Are There

Basel

The Uganda Plan

Imagine that you are at the Sixth Zionist Congress and the Uganda Plan is being debated. You are alarmed by the immediate danger under which many European Jews are living, especially in Russia where pogroms are a constant threat. Would you support the establishment of a Jewish home in East Africa? Or would you insist that the Jewish homeland be in the Land of Israel? Why?

_____

_____

_____

But many Zionists believed that creating a modern Jewish culture in the historic Jewish homeland was essential to the Jewish people's survival. None was more passionate than Asher Ginsberg, a gifted Russian Jewish writer who was known by his pen name, Aḥad Ha'am, meaning "One of the People." Aḥad Ha'am believed that Jews needed to return to their historic center—the Land of Israel, *Eretz Yisrael*—and develop a modern, secular Jewish culture that would bring unity to the Jewish people.

Aḥad Ha'am knew that many Jews would remain in the Diaspora even if a Jewish homeland was created. He believed that a Jewish homeland and national culture would enable

Diaspora Jewry to survive and flourish: "From [the Jewish] center [in Palestine] the spirit of Judaism will go forth...to all the communities of the Diaspora, and will breathe new life into them and preserve their unity."

The Second Aliyah

A new wave of immigrants arrived from Russia from 1905 to 1914. Called the **Second Aliyah**, it was driven by deadly pogroms in 1903 and a failed anti-czarist revolution in 1905. It had a powerful effect on the *Yishuv*, which is what the Zionist community in Palestine came to be called. (The Hebrew word *yishuv* means

25

Warning: Danger Ahead

Despite his passionate support of a Jewish state in the Land of Israel, Aḥad Ha'am voiced his deep concern that Palestine's majority Arab population would be hostile to Zionism.

Most Zionists ignored his concern. They convinced themselves that the Arabs would welcome the Jews. They expected the Arabs to be grateful to the Jews for bringing modern European culture to Palestine, including new technology and cures for diseases. The Zionists failed to imagine that the Arabs might develop their own nationalist feelings and resent becoming a minority in a land they, too, considered theirs.

While the Jewish population remained relatively small, few Arabs focused on the threat Zionism might pose for them. But as the Jewish population grew, Aḥad Ha'am's warning of conflict increasingly became a major concern.

"settlement.") Many of Israel's future leaders, including its first prime minister, David Ben-Gurion, and its second president, Yitzḥak ben Zvi, arrived during this period. Many came with only knapsacks on their backs and dreams of a just and modern Jewish state in their minds.

Unlike the earlier wave of immigrants, those who arrived during the Second Aliyah were committed to Socialist ideals. They dreamed of building up *Eretz Yisrael* with their own hands and experimented with new forms of cooperative living and farming.

A key figure in the Second Aliyah was Aaron David Gordon, who arrived in Palestine in 1904. Gordon believed that life in the Diaspora had made the Jews weak because it had disconnected them from the soil. He wanted to create a modern Jewish society in *Eretz Yisrael.* Gordon believed that manual labor would not only help strengthen the Jews, it would also enable them to rebuild their culture. He insisted that pioneers rely solely on "Hebrew

The Revival of Hebrew

From the moment Eliezer Perelman arrived in Jerusalem in 1882, he devoted himself to reviving Hebrew as a spoken language. First he changed his last name from Perelman to Ben-Yehuda. Next he persuaded his wife, Deborah, that they should speak only Hebrew in their home. Their eldest son, Ben-Tziyon (meaning "son of Zion"), is said to have been the first Hebrew-speaking child in modern history.

Ben-Yehuda realized that Hebrew had to be modernized if it was to be used in daily life. He spent years developing new Hebrew vocabulary to describe modern times. When possible, he constructed new words by using the roots of older, related words. For example, he created the modern Hebrew word *rakevet,* which means "train," from the root letters of the ancient Hebrew word for chariot.

Unlike the governments in Western Europe, the czars refused to emancipate the Jews. So, greater numbers of Russian Jews than Western European Jews were motivated to support the creation of a Jewish state where they would be free.

Jews in Russia	Jews in Western Europe
◎ Laws restricted where Jews were permitted to live.	◎ Jews could choose where they lived.
◎ The Jews did not have the same rights as Christians.	◎ By the late nineteenth century, the Jews had equal rights in many countries.
◎ The Jews were plagued by pogroms.	◎ Antisemitism was reduced for a while.

labor" rather than hiring Arabs. Gordon and the pioneers of the Second Aliyah were trying to create "new Jews," Jews who would disprove the antisemitic stereotypes of weakness.

The newcomers acquired new lands to settle and cultivate by turning to the **Jewish National Fund (JNF).** Created in 1901, the JNF bought land in Palestine to be owned by the entire Jewish people.

While this "back to the soil" movement inspired some of the new immigrants, many others settled in the cities. By 1908 the largely Arab port city of Jaffa was home to more than six thousand Jews. In 1909, with the help of the JNF, a group of settlers bought some nearby sand dunes and began construction. In time, a city was built and became known as Tel Aviv, meaning "Hill of the Spring"—a name that came from Ezekiel 3:15 and suggested rebirth. Just five years later, Tel Aviv had over two thousand residents.

Most of the approximately fifteen thousand immigrants who came during the Second Aliyah soon became disillusioned and left Palestine. Daily life was extremely harsh for those who remained. Food and other necessities were meager, and health conditions risky. Gordon's wife was one of many who died of malaria.

Children's Forest in Israel יער הילדים

In Honor Of
Michael Wasserman
MAZAL TOV ON YOUR BAR MITZVAH!

Planted By
Harry and Fred
Wasserman

JEWISH NATIONAL FUND   קרן קימת לישראל

Today, JNF certificates like this are sent to people who have been honored with the planting of a tree in Israel.

This photograph shows the founders of Tel Aviv in the spring of 1909, when the modern city was only a dream.

Many of the pioneers remained single and childless during their first years in the *Yishuv*. Their idealism and energies were focused on working the land and building up political organizations and unions.

Like these women, many of the pioneers were committed to working the land. A popular folk song summed up their goals: "We've come to this Land to build and to be rebuilt by it." What do you think these lyrics mean?

Foundation for the Future

In just a few decades Zionists built a solid movement and established over forty agricultural colonies and villages in the Land of Israel. The Jewish population of Palestine had grown to about sixty thousand—a little less than 10 percent of the total population. Hebrew was reborn as a language for daily life, and the young suburb of Tel Aviv was well on its way to becoming the first modern Jewish city.

But of all the Jews who left Russia from 1881 to 1914, only about 3 percent moved to Palestine. For the majority, Zionism and the Land of Israel were not a solution to the problems of economic hardship, antisemitism, and lack of political freedom. For them, it was the United States—not Palestine—that was the land of promise.

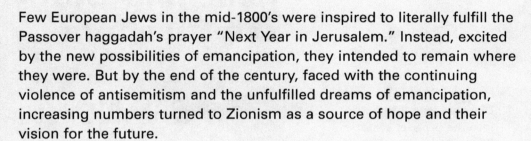

then & NOW

Few European Jews in the mid-1800's were inspired to literally fulfill the Passover haggadah's prayer "Next Year in Jerusalem." Instead, excited by the new possibilities of emancipation, they intended to remain where they were. But by the end of the century, faced with the continuing violence of antisemitism and the unfulfilled dreams of emancipation, increasing numbers turned to Zionism as a source of hope and their vision for the future.

1. Do you think that creating a Jewish state in the Land of Israel was a good solution to the problem of antisemitism? Why or why not?

_____

_____

2. Today, most Jews live in democratic countries where they are free to live as they want without fear of antisemitism. Do you think there is still a need for a Jewish state? Why or why not?

_____

_____

3. Just as Jews differed in their opinions about what the Jewish state should be like in the time of Herzl and Gordon, today Jews both in Israel and in the Diaspora often disagree on what the Jewish state should be like.

How might the difference of opinions benefit the Jewish people?

_____

_____

Why might the difference of opinions be a problem?

_____

_____

Chapter 4 World War I
Reaching Out Across the Diaspora

investigate

- How did World War I help Diaspora Jews integrate into the broader societies in which they lived?

- What impact did the war have on the spirit and the progress of the Zionist movement?

- How did American Jews help Jews in other countries rebuild their lives after the war?

- Do American Jews continue to feel the responsibility to help other Jews?

Key Words

Allied Powers	Bolsheviks
Central Powers	Communists
American Jewish Joint Distribution Committee (JDC)	Balfour Declaration

The BIG Picture

Like the pogroms in Russia in 1881 and 1882, World War I changed the face of world Jewry. Fought from 1914 to 1918, it was the largest and deadliest war the world had ever known. More than one and a half million Jewish soldiers served in the war; 177,000 of them died. Another four million Jews lay directly in the path of the marching armies. Hundreds of thousands of Jews were forced to flee their homes, and centuries-old European Jewish communities were destroyed.

Caught on both sides of the conflict, Jews demonstrated their desire to fit into their native lands by joining the armed forces of the country in which they lived. Thus, Jews would serve in the militaries of the United States and of Germany, among others, and would face one another as enemies on the battlefield.

After the war, as a result of the destruction European Jewry suffered, American Jewry held a new position of leadership in Jewish life, and England announced its support for the establishment of "a national home for the Jewish people" in the Land of Israel. In addition, in many parts of Europe the search for scapegoats led to an ominous rise in antisemitism.

1911	1914	1915
World History: Manchus overthrown; Sun Yat-sen elected provisional president of new Chinese republic	World War I begins	Joseph Trumpeldor persuades British officers to form all-Jewish fighting unit

Caught in the Fighting

World War I was fought between the **Allied Powers**—the United States, Russia, France, and Great Britain—and the **Central Powers,** led by Germany, Austria-Hungary, and the Ottoman Empire. From the start, a great wave of patriotism spread over European Jewry. To prove themselves devoted and loyal citizens, they joined the armed forces of their native countries in record numbers. National loyalties proved stronger than the ties linking Jews to one another.

If you were a young German Jew, you easily could have found yourself facing Jews from Russia on the battlefield. About 100,000 Jews served in the German army. As many as 650,000 Jews may have served in the Russian army. There were even two all-Jewish units in the British army: the Zion Mule Corps and the Jewish Legion.

1916

Louis D. Brandeis becomes first Jewish U.S. Supreme Court justice

1917

Communists seize control of Russia; British government expresses approval of creation of Jewish homeland in Palestine

1918

Allies win World War I; British take control of Palestine

All-Jewish Fighting Forces

When World War I broke out there had not been an all-Jewish army since the Bar Kochba Revolt against Rome nineteen hundred years before. Then, in 1915, Joseph Trumpeldor persuaded British officers to form a Jewish fighting unit. Trumpeldor was a Russian Jew who had lost his left arm in the 1904 war between Russian and Japan. Now he became part of the all-Jewish Zion Mule Corps, and was wounded again in fierce fighting against the Turks at Gallipoli.

Another Zionist leader from Russia, Ze'ev (Vladimir) Jabotinsky, helped form the Jewish Legion. Jewish Legion soldiers fought alongside the British as they drove the Turks out of Palestine. After the war, Trumpeldor, Jabotinsky, and many other Jewish veterans settled in Palestine. They formed the core of the fighting force that would one day defend the modern State of Israel.

How might the experience of forming their own fighting units in World War I have given the Jews an advantage later on in defending Israel?

_____

_____

As you can imagine, many Jews felt uncomfortable fighting for the Russian czar when so many Russian Jews were being persecuted. But in the spring of 1917, the czar was overthrown. The new government granted Jews full legal equality. Those who had opposed fighting side by side with Russia became more open to that possibility.

At the same time, millions of Jewish civilians were caught in the middle of the fighting. Hundreds of small, close-knit Jewish communities, or shtetls, were destroyed. Hundreds of thousands of Jews became wartime refugees—uprooted, without food, jobs, and shelter—and many became widows and orphans.

About 250,000 Jews fought in the U.S. military. Jewish chaplains became religious leaders, helping the Jewish soldiers celebrate Jewish holidays and giving them Jewish Bibles and prayer books. Close battlefield contact between Christians and Jews, as well as the heroic actions of Jewish soldiers, helped lessen negative stereotypes and inspired greater trust between the two groups.

Soldiers of the Jewish Legion next to the Western Wall in Jerusalem

Jewish soldiers from Austria, Hungary, and Poland at a prayer service

Despite the hardships of the war, communities continued to observe Jewish traditions and holidays. These men are carrying a barrel of boiling water through the streets of Lodz as they prepare to kosher dishes for Passover.

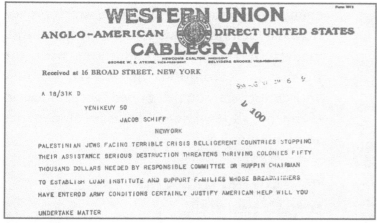

This cable was sent by the U.S. ambassador requesting help for the Jews of Palestine in 1914. It was the first appeal for aid and resulted in the founding of the JDC.

"The Joint"

With so many European communities destroyed, the American Jewish community stepped into a position of leadership. American Jews quickly formed three relief organizations. One represented the mostly American-born Reform Jews of Central European descent. A second was formed by Orthodox Jews, mostly East European in origin. And a third was organized by trade union leaders and Socialists who represented poor immigrant Jews who sought to help but could afford only small donations.

Pooling their funds, the money from all three organizations was distributed through a committee that became known as "the Joint"—the American Jewish Joint Distribution Committee (JDC). It was a great example of Jews of different backgrounds pooling their resources to achieve greater success together than they could have by acting separately.

Use the Internet or library resources to find out what the JDC does today. Record your findings here.

_____

_____

_____

A JDC committee meeting for a children's summer camp, 1919. Why might a camp be an important project for a charitable organization?

The War's Aftermath

World War I ended on November 11, 1918, with the defeat of Germany. European Jewry was greatly weakened—Eastern Europe was particularly devastated. Many Jews in Russia and Poland remained deep in poverty long afterward. They were kept alive only by donations from generous Diaspora Jews, especially those in America.

The czarist government of Russia had been overthrown, but the regime that replaced it did not last long. Under the leadership of Vladimir Ilich Lenin, **Bolsheviks,** or radical Russian **Communists,** seized control in the Revolution in 1917. (Communists believe in a social, economic, and political system that seeks to eliminate all private property in favor of a more equal distribution of resources among the population.) A brutal civil war followed the revolution, with the Bolshevik Red Army battling the anti-Bolshevik White Army.

While most Jewish organizations did not support Lenin, many Bolshevik leaders were Jewish. For opponents of the Bolsheviks, this provided an easy excuse for antisemitic attacks. Claiming that all Jews were Bolsheviks, the White Army butchered tens of thousands of Jews in pogroms. Communist supporters also murdered Jews—particularly those whom they considered "enemies of the people." Imagine: Jews were murdered both because they were considered Communists and because they were considered anti-Communists.

In Germany, meanwhile, some leaders blamed Jews for their country's defeat in the war. Antisemites charged that Jews were weak and that they had refused to fight for their country—contradicting the facts, which proved that many German Jews fought, died, and won medals in the war. In addition, with the Bolshevik Revolution in Russia, a new antisemitic stereotype gained acceptance in Germany: all Jews were seen as revolutionaries and Communists.

"A National Home for the Jewish People"

Increasingly it became clear that Jews needed a refuge, a place of protection where they could

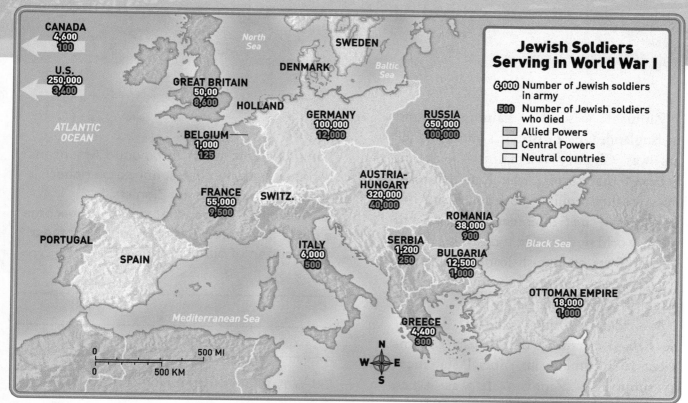

During World War I, Jews across Europe and North America fought for their home countries: about 1,250,000 for the Allied Powers and 500,000 for the Central Powers. On each side, about 1 of every 10 Jewish soldiers died.

defend themselves from antisemitic attack. Zionists were determined to create that refuge in the historic Jewish homeland, the Land of Israel.

Louis D. Brandeis boosted the Zionist cause. One of America's most famous and respected lawyers, Brandeis became a leader of the Zionist movement in 1914, tirelessly traveling around the United States to speak in support of Zionism. In 1916, he became the first Jewish Supreme Court justice. Brandeis won many new supporters, helping to make Zionism a strong political force in the United States. His commitment to Zionism especially influenced those American Jews who had feared that supporting the Zionist cause might imply that their loyalties were divided between America and the Jewish homeland. No one would question the loyalty of a great American like Brandeis.

Supreme Court Justice Louis D. Brandeis

Zionism was also gaining ground in England. One of Britain's Zionist leaders was Chaim Weizmann. Weizmann believed that turning the Zionist dream into a reality required both practical work in Palestine *and* diplomatic efforts with major world powers. He focused his diplomatic efforts on British leaders, believing them to be the most likely to support the establishment of a Jewish state.

Weizmann's strategy paid off. In 1917 he helped persuade the British government to formulate an official statement in support of Zionism. It was issued on November 2, 1917. The **Balfour Declaration,** as it came to be known, was a turning point in the history of the Zionist movement. It declared: "His Majesty's Government views with favor the establishment in Palestine of a national home for the Jewish people, and will use their best endeavors to facilitate the achievement of this object."

At first the British were not able to follow through on their promise—Palestine was still in the hands of Ottomans. But a month later, Britain forced the Turks out of Palestine and took control of the land.

The Ottoman Empire had sided with Germany and the Allied Powers had blockaded Palestine and prohibited trade. The coming of the British, especially given their promise of a "national home for the Jewish people," was seen as a hopeful sign for Palestine in general and for the Jews in particular.

What Do You Think?

Louis Brandeis said: "To be good Americans we must be better Jews, and to be better Jews, we must become Zionists."

Describe one way that striving to become a better Jew could help someone become a good citizen of our country.

_____

_____

_____

Why might being a Zionist make someone a better Jew?

_____

_____

_____

But the collapse of the Ottoman Empire had far-reaching negative effects on the 750,000 or so Jews who lived under Turkish and Arab rule. The Turkish city of Salonika, home to 80,000 Jews in 1900, fell to Greece in 1912 and was devastated by fire five years later. Tens of thousands of its Jews emigrated following World War I. Arab communities from Morocco to Iraq came under European control, and the Jews of Syria and Iraq suffered greatly during the transition. Most important, World War I inspired Arab nationalism, the hope that Arab

Chaim Weizmann

The son of a timber merchant, Chaim Weizmann (1874–1952) was born in the Russian village of Motol. While attending a Jewish school, one of his teachers smuggled science books into the classroom and secretly taught science—a subject that was frowned upon in many traditional Jewish communities. Weizmann discovered that he had a love and talent for science. He went on to study biochemistry in Germany and Switzerland and, after earning his doctorate, settled in England where he taught and made important discoveries in the field of chemistry.

Chaim Weizmann with his wife Vera

Weizmann's love of science was balanced with his passionate commitment to Zionism. He once said, "Miracles sometimes occur, but one has to work terribly hard for them." What did Weizmann mean?

_____

_____

Describe a "miracle" you want to occur. How might you help make it happen through your own hard work?

_____

_____

_____

nations could govern themselves. Arab nationalism and Jewish nationalism would soon come into conflict.

A New Jewish World

After World War I, Eastern Europe declined as a center of Jewish life, and the two new centers—the United States and the Land of Israel—gathered strength. The Jewish community of Palestine was still small. Yet it represented a place where persecuted Jews might settle and live in freedom. The Zionist movement continued to gain followers.

The American Jewish community became the second-largest Jewish community in the world—and by far the best organized, richest, and most powerful. (The largest Jewish community was in Russia.) American Jews began to play a critical role in world Jewish affairs, a role they continue to play to this day.

These two orphaned sisters were among the Russian refugees who arrived in Jaffa, Palestine, in 1921. They found shelter in an orphanage that was supported by the JDC.

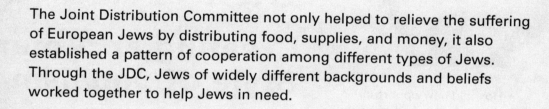

then & NOW

The Joint Distribution Committee not only helped to relieve the suffering of European Jews by distributing food, supplies, and money, it also established a pattern of cooperation among different types of Jews. Through the JDC, Jews of widely different backgrounds and beliefs worked together to help Jews in need.

1. Describe one way you can work with other Jews to help Jews in need.

_____

_____

_____

2. Helping other Jews does not free us from our responsibility to also help non-Jews. Describe one way you can work with other Jews to help non-Jews in need.

_____

_____

_____

3. How can your Jewish identity be strengthened by working with other Jews to help people in need?

_____

_____

_____

Chapter 5 At Home in the U.S., 1920–1940

Creating an American Style of Judaism

investigate

- How did new opportunities and new challenges change life for American Jews in the 1920's and 1930's?

- What new forms of Jewish life and worship were developed?

- How did the Jews of this time contribute to today's American Jewish community?

Key Words

Quotas	Reconstructionism
Yeshivas	Great Depression

The BIG Picture

From 1880 to 1920, the Jewish population of the United States leaped from 250,000 to three and a half million. This explosive growth was largely due to the massive wave of Jewish immigration from Eastern Europe. But in the early 1920's, anti-immigration feelings began rising and, in response, Congress set strict limits on the number of immigrants allowed into America, particularly from Eastern and Southern Europe.

With the doors of immigration almost completely shut by Congress in 1924, native-born Jews soon outnumbered those Jews who had been born outside the United States. The typical Jew was now someone who was on the way to blending into the American middle class while having a strong Jewish identity based largely on ethnic ties. Such Jews were called "alrightniks." As more Jews became integrated into American society, they began to personalize their religious practices and develop a uniquely American style of Judaism.

1920
U.S. Jewish population reaches 3.5 million

1921
World History:
Canadian researchers Frederick Banting and Charles Herbert Best discover insulin, the life-saving treatment for diabetes

1922
First public bat mitzvah ceremony held in U.S.

1924
Immigration Act of 1924 limits immigration to U.S. from Eastern and Southern Europe

$100,00

אדאקשאן

אנֶענֶר פֿן אָנֿפֿאַנֶג

ביז ענֶדֶע

רֶעֶסֶטֶע אֶן

עֶסֶאַנֶטֶסֶטֶע

אֶיֶדֶר האָט

ג עֶזֶעֶהֶן

ﬠﬡﬢﬦﬤﬥ אֶ יֶﬠﬤﬡ﬩

פֿרָאַדֶוֹסֶיֶרֶטֶן

סֶטֶ סֶיֶיֶק

SIDE SAD

A Jewish-American First

"No thunder sounded, no lightning struck," noted Judith Kaplan Eisenstein recalling her bat mitzvah celebration on March 18, 1922. It was an historic day: the first public bat mitzvah ceremony in the United States. Judith's father was Rabbi Mordecai Kaplan, a professor at the Conservative movement's Jewish Theological Seminary (JTS). Kaplan was committed to advancing the religious equality of women. One way was to conduct a bat mitzvah ceremony for his daughter in his new synagogue in New York City, The Society for the Advancement of Judaism.

1926
National Council on Jewish Education formed to improve quality of Jewish education in U.S.

1927
Henry Ford apologizes for printing antisemitic articles in his newspaper

1929
Stock market crash leads to Great Depression in U.S.

1937
Reform rabbis formally support building Jewish homeland in Palestine and reintroduce more traditional Jewish rituals

The Pressure of Being First

Judith Kaplan was not as eager as her father to be a pioneer. As an adult, she remembered having had mixed feelings, "being perfectly willing to defy my grandmothers [who opposed the ceremony], pleased to have a somewhat flattering attention paid me, and yet perturbed by the possible effect this might have on the attitude of my own peers, the early teenagers who…could be remarkably cruel to the 'exception,' to the non-conformist."

Do you think that choosing to be the first girl in the United States to publicly celebrate becoming a bat mitzvah took courage on the part of Judith Kaplan? Why or why not?

_____

_____

How can prayer or other Jewish traditions give you courage when you need to make difficult choices?

_____

_____

Rose Schneiderman, the daughter of poor Jewish immigrants, was a garment worker, a leading union organizer, and a feminist. Her influence went as far as the White House, where she was befriended by President Franklin Roosevelt and his wife, Eleanor. Schneiderman is seen here speaking at a women's suffrage meeting.

identities. Their many strategies included Americanizing Judaism itself. Thus, just as American women gained political power when they won the right to vote in 1920, so Judith and her father helped Jewish women take a step in gaining religious equality in 1922.

Moving on Up

The economic status of American Jews improved along with that of millions of other Americans during the country's economic boom in the 1920's. This did not mean overnight middle-class comfort for new immigrants. But many of their children were able to take advantage of the educational and economic opportunities in America, entering professions such as teaching, law, and medicine.

Jews also started their own businesses, especially in new and growing industries like

Although public bat mitzvah ceremonies were not widely conducted until the 1960's, Judith Kaplan helped set the wheels in motion. She did so at a time when Jews were trying hard to Americanize yet hold on to their Jewish

The Early Americanization of Judaism

Throughout Jewish history, Jews have adapted Judaism to the times and places in which they have lived. They had been adapting Judaism to American life since at least the American Revolution. Beginning in Charleston in 1825, under the influence of Reform Judaism, the pace of change quickened.

Reform Jews believed that Judaism had to adapt to survive. Thus, they introduced innovations such as English-language prayers, mixed seating of men and women, and organ music. The goal was to make Judaism less foreign and more meaningful and uplifting to Americans. By making Judaism more compatible with the American way of life, it was hoped that young, American-born Jews would be attracted to it. Some even thought prayer services should be modeled after the style of Protestant worship.

Those who did not share the views of the Reform—whether they called themselves "Orthodox," "Conservative," or "Traditional" Jews—insisted that Jews must uphold and maintain Judaism's sacred religious traditions in order to survive. While they agreed that Jewish worship should be dignified and they accepted certain innovations, such as the English-language sermon, they drew the line when it came to changing Jewish law. Judaism's future, they believed, depended on the education and uplifting of American Jews, not on changes to the core of Jewish practice and belief.

music, radio, and movies. Young Jewish composers, such as George Gershwin and Irving Berlin, were among the most popular songwriters in America. A pioneer of the radio industry, David Sarnoff established the first national radio network, the National Broadcasting Company (NBC), in 1926. And in Hollywood, Jews founded most of the major American movie studios.

The Rabbi's Family was performed in 1921 at the People's Theatre in New York City. By 1929, American Jews were enjoying silent Yiddish movies, like *East Side Sadie,* and by 1937 Yiddish "talkies," like *Where Is My Child?*

Judaism American Style

As Jews increasingly became middle class and more Americanized, they reshaped Judaism. Think about the evolution of the bar mitzvah celebration. It was once a simple synagogue ritual in which a thirteen-year-old boy was called to the Torah for the first time. Then, in the 1960's, bat mitzvah ceremonies also became popular in many American communities. Today, some adults who did not have a bar or bat mitzvah ceremony as teenagers participate in adult versions of the ritual.

Over time, the celebratory parties have become much more elaborate than they once were, complete with catered food and live entertainment. Today, many synagogues focus on the religious significance of becoming a bar or bat mitzvah by requiring students to participate in mitzvah projects, such as collecting food and clothing for the poor.

In the years after World War I, American Jews transformed not only life-cycle events, but also the celebration of Jewish holidays. For instance, with its theme of freedom, Passover held great meaning to American Jews. The holiday soon became the most observed festival on the Jewish calendar. In time, big companies began advertising directly to Jewish customers and manufacturing a variety of kosher foods, influencing Jewish life and observance.

Describe one possible advantage of the Americanization of Judaism.

_____

_____

Describe one possible disadvantage of the Americanization of Judaism.

_____

_____

Portrait of twins commemorating their bar mitzvah celebration (1927)

Old Problems in a New Land

Even as the Jews were successfully adapting to life in America, familiar problems arose. Although antisemitism was not as strong or as dangerous in America as it was in Europe, it did become more widespread after World War I. Prejudice intensified in some Americans, especially in lower-middle-class communities in small towns. They felt that their way of life was threatened, that immigrant Jews (and Catholics) were destroying American society.

America was changing quickly, becoming more urban, more culturally diverse, and more

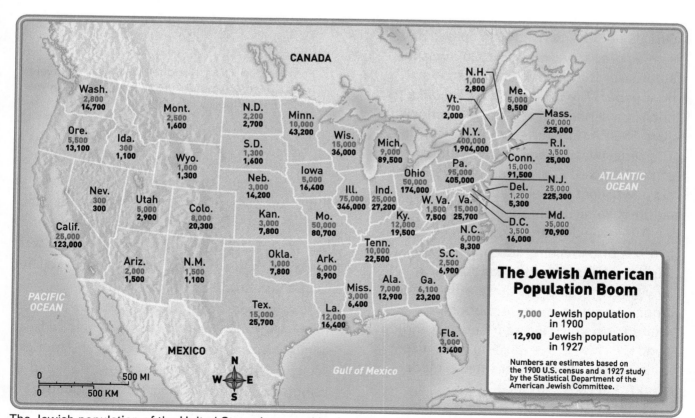

The Jewish American Population Boom

7,000	Jewish population in 1900
12,900	Jewish population in 1927

Numbers are estimates based on the 1900 U.S. census and a 1927 study by the Statistical Department of the American Jewish Committee.

The Jewish population of the United States increased by four times between 1900 and 1927, from 1,000,000 to more than 4,000,000. Interestingly, the Jewish population of Canada increased by more than seven times during that time, from 20,000 to 150,000.

involved in the affairs of the world. As small-town Americans watched their familiar way of life slipping away, many wanted to turn back the clock. They accused the Jews in the entertainment industry of producing movies and writing songs designed to destroy traditional American culture and values. They imagined that the Jews were secretly trying to bring about a Communist revolution in the United States, yet also believed that the Jews controlled major capitalist interests.

Henry Ford and Antisemitism

One powerful American who spread anti-semitic propaganda in the 1920's was the automaker Henry Ford. Ford used his newspaper, *The Dearborn Independent,* to publish a series called "The International Jew: The World's Foremost Problem." The series was based on *The Protocols of the Elders of Zion.* Ford made sure that his newspaper was available at all of his automobile dealerships.

American Jewish leaders took action. In 1927, under economic and legal pressure, Ford apologized to the American Jewish community for these articles and stopped printing them. Although he offered Jews his "future friendship and good will," he never gave up his antisemitic beliefs. He even accepted a medal from Adolf Hitler.

Ford's antisemitic series of articles, which appeared in *The Dearborn Independent,* led to a mass boycott of Ford automobiles by American Jews.

Antisemitism was not confined to small-town America. Many universities set **quotas,** or limits, on the number of Jews who could enroll in their schools, and many businesses refused to hire Jews. Certain wealthy neighborhoods were made off-limits to Jews, and Jews were excluded from many social clubs and resorts.

Jews responded to antisemitism in a variety of ways. Some sought to escape their Judaism completely and melt into the larger American society. Others adopted strategies designed to minimize or mask their Jewish identity in public. Changing one's name was one way to do this. The actress Betty Persky, for example, became Lauren Bacall. Songwriter Israel Baline, who composed two of America's best-known holiday classics, "White Christmas" and "Easter Parade," became Irving Berlin.

But, generally, Jews simply found ways around the challenges of antisemitism. When quotas prevented Jews from enrolling in private universities, they turned to schools without quotas. Brandeis University was founded in 1948, in part as a response to quotas that denied Jews entrance into elite universities. Rather than try to earn a living in companies that did not welcome them, many Jews started their own businesses, law firms, and medical practices. Similarly, they also created their own country clubs and vacation resorts.

"Jewishness" Without Judaism

Many Jews imagined that the move to middle-class neighborhoods would lead to greater interaction with non-Jews. For the most part, however, they were wrong. As Jews moved in, white Protestants moved out. In many cases, their new communities became as Jewish or more heavily Jewish than the neighborhoods they had left. Signs of "Jewishness" were everywhere—from potato knishes to Yiddish newspaper vendors, from storefront synagogues to corner delicatessens.

Many Jews had given up attending synagogue and strictly observing Jewish laws and rituals. In 1919, less than a quarter of American Jews were members of a synagogue, and many limited their attendance to High Holidays and the anniversaries of family members' deaths. Many expressed their Jewish identities by taking part in cultural activities, such as Yiddish theater and concerts, or by engaging in political activism, like organizing labor unions or Zionist clubs. The popularity of Jewish secularism alarmed religious leaders. Most agreed that Judaism urgently needed to respond to the challenges posed by American life and become meaningful to the upwardly mobile American Jews.

Americanization of Jewish Religious Life

As the twentieth century progressed, more and more East European Jews found a home in the Reform movement. By 1931, half of the Reform synagogues' membership traced their roots to Eastern Europe. In 1937, Reform rabbis adopted a new platform that supported building a Jewish homeland in Palestine. The platform also supported the reintroduction of more traditional Jewish rituals and ceremonies. Bar mitzvah ceremonies were reintroduced, as was the use of Hebrew in prayer services.

But most American Jews of East European origin found Reform Judaism too foreign to adopt. Instead, some adapted Orthodox Judaism to American life. In 1928, they opened the upper Manhattan campus of Yeshiva College, which emphasized secular as well as Jewish studies. These modern Orthodox Jews were likely to discuss sports scores and the latest movies as well as the weekly Torah portion. Only the most strictly Orthodox resisted American culture. In their effort to do so, they built up a network of **yeshivas,** Orthodox schools, designed to carry on traditional learning and Old World values.

The fastest-growing movement during this period was the Conservative movement. In 1919 only 22 congregations identified themselves as Conservative. By 1929 the number had jumped to 229. The Conservative movement generally steered a middle course. Balancing tradition and change, it embraced the traditional order and form of prayer services while accepting innovations such as seating men and women together during the services.

Most teachers at the Conservative movement's Jewish Theological Seminary were primarily concerned with maintaining Conservative Judaism's commitment to Jewish law and tradition. An important exception was Rabbi Mordecai Kaplan who believed that Judaism would not survive unless it was adapted to American life and values. In keeping with this conviction, he rejected the traditional idea of the Jews as "the chosen people" claiming that it conflicted with American ideals of democracy and equality.

Influenced by modern scientific advances, Kaplan viewed God as a force or power for good but not as a supernatural being capable of reversing the laws of nature on performing miracles. He saw the Torah as sacred but not as a literal record of God's words to Moses. And he believed that in America, Jews live in two

Kid-Friendly Judaism

As Judaism Americanized, it also became more child-centered. Synagogue sisterhoods taught mothers how to make their homes more Jewish and how to capture the interest of their children with Jewish-themed games, activities, and special foods—from instructions on how to make Bible dolls to recipes for Maccabean sandwiches. Jewish children's books also became more common, and the celebration of Ḥanukkah became increasingly widespread as an alternative to Christmas.

Efforts were also made to modernize afternoon religious schools, the Talmud Torahs. In the first decades of the twentieth century, many boys were receiving little more than bar mitzvah training, while girls rarely received any Jewish education. With the help of Mordecai Kaplan, Samson Benderly led an effort to develop schools that taught about an American style of Jewish life. Students sang Jewish songs, learned about Jewish current events, and created Jewish art projects and cultural presentations. In addition, they learned about Zionist culture and how to read and speak modern Hebrew.

Mordecai Kaplan

Mordecai Kaplan

Mordecai Kaplan (1881–1983) was born into an Orthodox family in Lithuania. When he was eight-years-old, he and his family moved to New York City. As a teenager, influenced by both secular and religious studies, Kaplan saw Judaism in a new way. After completing his university studies, he was ordained as a Conservative rabbi.

Zionism was central to Kaplan's vision of Judaism. He saw Palestine as the birthplace of Jewish civilization. By civilization, Kaplan meant everything from Jewish religion to Jewish music, art, literature, and food. He believed that a strong and creative Jewish civilization in the Diaspora along with an equally thriving Jewish civilization in the Land of Israel would help Judaism develop and grow.

Rather than believing that Jewish law was absolute, he was famous for saying, "*Halachah* [Jewish law] should have a vote but not a veto." Kaplan taught that each Jew must study Jewish tradition in order to figure out what it means to him or her to be a Jew.

Describe what being a Jew means to you.

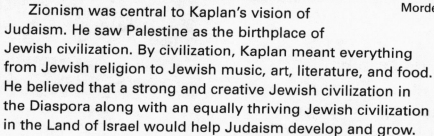

Based on what being a Jew means to you, describe one action or mitzvah that particularly reflects your Jewish identity. Explain why.

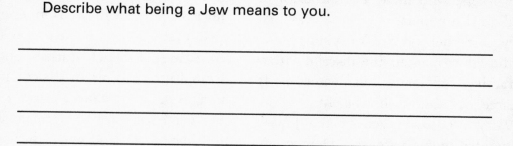

civilizations, one reflecting American traditions and ways of life and the other reflecting Jewish traditions and ways of life.

Kaplan's system of ideas and beliefs, which he called **Reconstructionism,** influenced many Reform, Orthodox, and especially, Conservative Jews. Reconstructionism remained within Conservative Judaism until after World War II when it became a movement like Conservative and Reform Judaism. The Reconstructionist Rabbinical College was founded in 1968.

Politics and World Events

The **Great Depression** in the 1930's caused many hardships, including unemployment and poverty, and the Jews suffered along with all other Americans. With the failure of the New York Bank of the United States, many Jews saw their life savings all but disappear. Jewish garment workers, who made up one-third of New York's Jewish population, were devastated when they lost their jobs. For young Jews entering the labor market, the discriminatory hiring practices of many businesses made already scarce jobs almost nonexistent.

The 1930's also saw much of the Jewish community identifying with the Democratic Party. Most Jews supported President Franklin D. Roosevelt's New Deal policies, which created programs to give relief, create jobs, and stimulate economic recovery for the United States. Many felt a personal connection with Roosevelt, because he opened government jobs

Sign in English and Yiddish in a Jewish store during the Depression announcing that relief tickets could be exchanged for food. Can you find the phrase "relief tickets" in Yiddish?

to Jews and had an unusually large number of Jewish advisers within his inner circle.

But Jews were not able to convince Roosevelt to ease the strict quotas on immigration from Europe. This was becoming an issue of increasing importance, because Adolf Hitler had come to power in Germany and conditions for Jews in Poland and other East European countries were also worsening. American Jews responded to the declining conditions by supporting the building up of the Jewish homeland and the resettlement of refugees in Palestine. Membership in Zionist organizations grew rapidly in the mid- to late 1930's.

then & NOW

Jews were beginning to feel more like Americans by the 1930's, and this was reflected in their synagogues, called *shuls* in Yiddish. East European congregations with Yiddish-speaking rabbis increasingly hired English-speaking associate rabbis who could preach to younger members who did not understand Yiddish. Rabbis like Herbert Goldstein and Mordecai Kaplan also popularized the concept of the synagogue center, the "shul with a pool." This new synagogue center expanded the programs of the traditional synagogue to include educational and social activities, and even athletic facilities. Multipurpose synagogue buildings were built in Jewish communities all over the United States.

1. Do you think it is appropriate for a synagogue to have a gym or social activities and facilities, such as a Purim carnival or teen recreation room? Why or why not?

_____

_____

2. In the space below, draw a floor plan for your ideal synagogue. Label each area to describe what you would include, such as a sanctuary, office, and religious school.

Chapter **6** The British Mandate

Zionist Achievements and Arab-Jewish Conflict

investigate

- In what ways were the Zionist settlers freer than they had been in Russia and Eastern Europe?

- How might that freedom have affected their identities as Jews?

- What were the causes of growing tensions between Jews and Arabs in British-ruled Palestine?

- What impact might the changing identity of the Jew in Palestine have had on the Jews of the Diaspora?

Key Words and Places

Mandates	Technion
Haganah	Hebrew University
Old City	Fourth Aliyah
New City	Youth Aliyah
Third Aliyah	Partition Plan
Ḥalutzim	White Paper
Kibbutzim	Irgun

The **BIG** Picture

On the morning of December 9, 1917, the residents of Jerusalem woke to find that their city had a new ruler. The British army, commanded by General Edmund Allenby, had defeated the Turks, and the British now controlled Jerusalem. Crowds of residents, both Jews and Arabs, flooded the streets and greeted the British as liberators.

A month earlier, Britain's Balfour Declaration had promised support for a Jewish homeland in Palestine. To many Jews, Britain's victory over the Turks and its promise to establish a Jewish national homeland seemed like a modern-day Ḥanukkah miracle.

A time of great growth and achievement was beginning for the Zionists of Palestine, and a new identity of the Jew as a courageous and powerful pioneer and soldier was developing. But it was also a period in which the seeds of conflict between the Jews and Arabs were sown.

1912	1914	1917	1919	1920
Henrietta Szold founds Hadassah, the Women's Zionist Organization of America	**World History:** Panama Canal opens, linking Atlantic and Pacific oceans	British army takes control of Jerusalem	Third Aliyah begins; brings 40,000 Jews to Palestine	Jews form Haganah to protect Zionist community of Palestine

The Roots of the Conflict

The Jews were not the only ones with high expectations. The Arabs, too, were filled with hope. The British had told them that they would receive an independent state in return for staging a revolt against the Turks. But the British had also signed a secret agreement with France in which each agreed to take a piece of the Ottoman Empire for itself, and jointly rule most of Palestine.

The British made these conflicting promises because they were determined to win the war with the Turks. They hoped their promises would gain the cooperation of the various groups. Their strategy worked, but when the war ended it became clear that Britain could not possibly keep all its promises.

Britain and France divided up the region much the way they had agreed. It was carved up into **mandates,** colony-like territories that Britain and France would govern until they determined that the population was ready for independence. The borders of the mandates were designed more to satisfy the interests of the British and the French than to address the needs and interests of the Arabs and Jews.

1924

Fourth Aliyah begins; brings 80,000 Jews to Palestine

1929

Arab riots throughout Palestine

1936

Palestinian Arabs begin the Great Uprising

1939

British issue White Paper, ending their commitment to the establishment of a Jewish homeland in Palestine

Hashomer (The Guard) was an organization responsible for the security of many Jewish settlements in Palestine from 1909 to 1920. All it required of the settlements was that they employ only Jewish workers.

The Arabs opposed the creation of mandates. They believed that the European powers had no right to rule over them. They also opposed the Balfour Declaration and the Zionist desire to build a Jewish nation in Palestine. Palestine, they argued, already had an Arab population and it had no desire to become a minority in a Jewish state.

The roots of the conflict over Palestine lie in the struggle between two peoples for the same small piece of land. Britain's effort to build a Jewish national home without raising Arab opposition was doomed from the start.

Violence Breaks Out

Violence between Jews and Arabs first flared in March 1920. Jews living in an isolated group of settlements in the far north of Palestine found themselves in the middle of a battle between Arab nationalists and French troops. Despite the Zionists' efforts to remain neutral, the Arabs were convinced that the Zionists were aiding the French.

Zionist leaders encouraged the settlers to leave the area. Many did, but the members of two settlements, Tel Ḥai and Kfar Gil'adi, chose to stay. On March 1 several hundred Arabs arrived at Tel Ḥai looking for hidden French soldiers. A firefight erupted. The settlers temporarily drove out the Arabs. But in the end, the settlers were forced to leave.

A month after this incident, anti-Jewish riots broke out in Jerusalem. Protesters descended on Jews with clubs, knives, and stones.

In the Diaspora, Jews had often seemed powerless and defenseless. Such memories troubled the "new Jews" of Palestine. They formed a militia called the **Haganah** (defense) to protect the *Yishuv*, the Zionist community in Palestine. Under the leadership of Ze'ev Jabotinsky, the

A Symbol of Courage

Despite the Tel Ḥai and Kfar Gil'adi defeats, the heroism of the settlers has become legendary. Among the dead was Joseph Trumpeldor, who had been committed to teaching Jews self-defense. At Tel Ḥai, he gave his life for this principle. In death, Trumpeldor became a larger-than-life hero and a symbol of courage. It is said that his final words were: "Never mind, it is good to die for our country."

Why do you think it was important for Zionists to have symbols of courage such as Joseph Trumpeldor?

_____

_____

_____

Haganah helped evacuate some Jewish families from the center of the rioting, the area in East Jerusalem known as the **Old City.** To ensure that the rioting did not spread, they also patrolled the streets of West Jerusalem, which is referred to as the **New City.**

The Pioneer Spirit

Another wave of Jewish immigration to Palestine occurred after World War I; it is known as the **Third Aliyah.** A core of these new immigrants was devoted to working the land and living Socialist ideals. They called themselves *ḥalutzim,* based on the biblical word for a frontline soldier or pioneer. In many ways, they followed in the footsteps of the Second Aliyah. They, too, were committed to "Hebrew labor," the Hebrew language, self-defense, and social justice.

The *ḥalutzim* set up the first settlements formally known as *kibbutzim,* villages in which a group lived and worked together, owned all property together, and kept its money in a common treasury. Many *kibbutzim* had factories as well as farms. Kibbutz members prided themselves on the equal treatment of men and women. Women held jobs as diverse as cooking, child rearing, driving tractors, and harvesting fruit.

By the late 1920's, about four thousand people lived on approximately thirty *kibbutzim.* A number were built in outlying areas to provide security and widen the borders of the growing Jewish national home. Although *kibbutzim* accounted for only a small percentage of the total Jewish population, they had a large impact on the *Yishuv.* Beyond their role in securing the land, many leading military figures, politicians, and intellectuals were drawn from *kibbutzim.*

The Labor Brigade

The pride of the Third Aliyah was the Joseph Trumpeldor Labor Brigade, named for Tel Ḥai's fallen hero. Almost two thousand *ḥalutzim* were members of the brigade at one time or another. The brigade hired itself out to new settlements. Its members built roads and drained swamps, living in tent camps and braving harsh conditions.

The Growth of Urban Jewish Centers

As in earlier years, the majority of Jewish immigrants settled in cities. In Haifa an entirely Jewish community, Hadar Hacarmel, was developed. By the mid-1920's, it had over three thousand residents and the **Technion,** an institute of technology, was opened. Both Jews and Arabs flocked to Haifa as its fortunes continued to rise in the 1930's, when the British built a modern port and completed an oil pipeline to Iraq.

Jerusalem, too, was growing. New middle-class Jewish neighborhoods were constructed in West Jerusalem. In East Jerusalem, Mount Scopus became the site of the **Hebrew University,** a center for Jewish scholarship.

The fastest-growing city by far was Tel Aviv. Between 1914 and 1939 its population exploded from 2,000 to 160,000. With its seaside promenade, sidewalk cafés, broad avenues, public squares, and neighborhood parks, Tel Aviv felt like a European city with a Mediterranean flavor. It became known for its modernity, sophistication, and secular Jewish culture.

Famous FIGURES

Henrietta Szold

Henrietta Szold

Baltimore-born Henrietta Szold (1860–1945) made her first visit to Palestine in 1909. Troubled by the unhealthy living conditions of the children there, Szold returned to the United States to form Hadassah, the Women's Zionist Organization of America. For the rest of her life, she worked to improve health care and education for Palestine's Jews and Arabs.

Hadassah sent American-trained nurses and, later, entire medical units to Palestine to combat the primitive health conditions. It worked to improve maternity and infant care, and set up training programs for nurses, as well as health clinics, and, later, hospitals.

Hadassah Hospital opened in Jerusalem in 1939. Today it is considered one of the finest hospitals in the Middle East. It continues Szold's commitment to providing quality medical care to Jews and Arabs.

Szold is also known for other life-saving work. After Hitler came to power in Germany in 1933, thousands of Jewish children from Germany were sent by their parents to Palestine. They were part of Youth Aliyah, a project directed by Szold to help young Jews escape from Germany. About five thousand teenagers arrived in Palestine before World War II, and more than fifteen thousand children came after the war.

Describe two Jewish values that may have inspired Szold's concern for both Jews and Arabs.

1. _____

2. _____

Hadassah's food donations provided critical support to this Yemenite kindergarten in Neveh Sha'anan, Jerusalem (1920).

Separate Lives

The **Fourth Aliyah,** which lasted from 1924 to 1928, brought another eighty thousand Jewish immigrants to Palestine, including middle-class shopkeepers and craftspeople. The Palestinian Arab population was growing quickly, too, mostly because the British improved health conditions, road and rail networks, and sewage systems. The decline of the rural economy brought many peasants to the cities. Urban Arabs created a rich intellectual and cultural life, and newspapers and political parties introduced many to the ideas of Arab nationalism.

Arabs and Jews often led separate lives, even in mixed cities like Haifa and Jaffa. Zionists created their own economy and cultural institutions, organizing their own trade union and priding themselves on hiring only Jews.

The 1929 Riots

The Arabs became alarmed as Jews bought up land. The Jewish National Fund preferred to buy areas that were uninhabited. But as such territory became scarce, Jews bought land from Arabs whose property was leased to other Arabs. Many tenants had lived on and farmed the land for generations. When the new, Jewish owners evicted them, it fueled Arab resentment.

Arab fears of a growing Jewish population buying more and more land set off a new round of riots in 1929. The worst violence took place in the cities of Safed and Hebron, where rioters attacked the Hebron yeshiva and Jewish homes. Sixty-six Jews were killed.

Jews in larger cities were better able to defend themselves. Haganah squads patrolled the streets and fired on rioters. The British army and police tried to put down the violence. Low-flying British aircraft even fired at a band of Arab villagers on their way to attack Jews in Haifa. But there were only 292 policemen and fewer than a hundred soldiers in all of Palestine. In total, 133 Jews and 116 Arabs were killed.

The riots convinced the high commissioner of Palestine that the Balfour Declaration was "a colossal blunder." He urged the British government to back away from its promises to the Jews. In London, British officials were beginning to wonder whether the mandate in Palestine was more trouble than it was worth.

The Arab Revolt

The rise to power of Adolf Hitler in Germany caused yet another wave of Jewish immigration to Palestine. Between 1933 and 1936, about 165,000 immigrants arrived from Europe. By 1936 Jews made up almost one-third of the entire population of Palestine. Jewish dreams and Arab fears of a Jewish majority in Palestine seemed on the verge of becoming a reality.

Despite the difficult times Hebrew culture managed to thrive. The Habimah Theater, which was founded in Russia in 1917 and was committed to producing plays in Hebrew, moved to Palestine in 1931. In 1945 it moved into a building in the heart of Tel Aviv and thirteen years later became the National Theater of Israel.

In 1936, these young pioneers waved good-bye to their friends and family as they set out from Berlin, Germany, for the long journey to Palestine and a new life.

In April 1936, an organized Arab revolt began, aimed at stopping the Zionist nation-building project and ending British rule. The Arabs declared a general strike. Shops were closed, and many Arabs refused to pay their taxes.

The Great Uprising, as the Palestinian Arabs called it, enjoyed popular support and mass participation among the Palestinian Arab population. Grand Mufti Haj Amin al-Husseini, who eventually took charge of the revolt, announced that the strike would end only when Jewish immigration was halted. Arab rebels bombed the oil pipeline, railway lines, and trains, assassinated British officials, and committed acts of terrorism against Jews. The British brought in twenty thousand troops and put down the rebellion.

The Partition Plan

In November 1936, a British commission, known as the Peel Commission, arrived in Palestine to determine the causes of the revolt and to recommend a solution. The commission spoke with both Jewish and Arab leaders, including Ben-Gurion, Weizmann, and al-Husseini. In July 1937 it issued a 404-page report concluding that Jews and Arabs could never live peacefully in one state. The only solution was a **partition plan** that would divide Palestine into two states.

The report suggested that the Jews receive the Galilee, the Jezreel Valley, and most of the coast. The Negev, the Gaza Strip, and the West Bank would be given to the Arabs. Jerusalem and some of the other towns with mixed Arab and Jewish populations would remain in British hands. The proposed map gave the Jews only one-fifth of Palestine but the leadership of the *Yishuv* accepted the plan, however reluctantly. In Weizmann's words, "The Jews would be fools not to accept it even if [the Jewish State] were the size of a tablecloth." The Arabs, however, rejected the idea of partition. In their minds, the only just solution to the Palestine problem was an independent, majority Arab state.

The White Paper

After a lull while the Peel Commission met, the revolt started again. The British stepped up their actions against the Arabs; by early 1939, the revolt collapsed. But the human toll of the uprising was enormous: over five thousand Arabs, five hundred Jews, and two hundred Britons were dead. Al-Husseini fled to Germany and supported the Nazis during World War II.

What, wondered the British government, was the solution to the Palestine problem? In Europe, the threat from Germany was rising and war seemed inevitable. Keeping twenty thousand troops in Palestine was out of the question. The British decided to withdraw the promises made in the Balfour Declaration. British leaders wanted to secure Arab cooperation in the coming conflict with Germany. They knew they could count on Jewish cooperation because the Zionists would want to help defend the Jews of Europe.

In May 1939, Britain issued its long-awaited **White Paper,** or official government report. Palestine, the White Paper declared, was to become an independent state allied with the British Empire. To assure that the Arabs remained a majority in Palestine, Jewish immigration was to be limited to seventy-five thousand over the next five years. Jewish immigration would then require Arab permission. Land sales to Jews also were severely restricted.

The Zionists were outraged. All they had worked for was at risk. They also were concerned about the fate of the Jews of Europe, who were endangered by Hitler's rise to power in Germany. With other countries enforcing strict immigration quotas, unrestricted immigration to Palestine seemed the best hope for saving the Jews of Germany and Eastern Europe.

The leaders of the *Yishuv* had a dilemma: they could no longer cooperate with the British authorities in Palestine, but they understood the importance of defeating Hitler, which required that they ally themselves with Britain. They decided to act on both concerns. Their policy was summed up by Ben-Gurion who declared, "We shall fight the war as if there were no White Paper and we shall fight the White Paper as if there were no war."

Arab and Jewish Population in Palestine 1914–1946

Year	Arab Population	Jewish Population
1914	738,000	60,000
1922	730,000	85,000
1931	880,000	175,000
1939	1,070,000	460,000
1946	1,269,000	608,000

You Are There

Palestine

The Haganah and Irgun Respond to Violence

Imagine you are living in Palestine during the Arab Revolt. The violence shocks the *Yishuv,* convincing many Jews that it is impossible to live with the Arabs.

You know that Ben-Gurion and other leaders of the *Yishuv* do not want to provoke the British. That is why, at first, the leadership followed a policy of restraint. In the early months of the revolt, most of the Haganah's actions were defensive, such as patrolling settlements. Jabotinsky's followers opposed the policy of restraint but their underground militia, the Irgun Tz'vei Leumi, known simply as the Irgun and headed by Menaḥem Begin, went along with that policy.

As Arab violence increases, many who had resisted taking up arms now believe that there is no alternative but to fight for the community's survival. Their rallying cry is *"Ein breirah!"* "There is no choice!" The British army and Haganah organize joint night squads, which ambush Arab fighters and attack the villages they use as bases. Irgun fighters conduct scores of attacks on Arab civilians in marketplaces, cafés, and buses, killing more than 250 people.

Do you agree or disagree with the decision to move away from the policy of restraint? Explain your reasons.

_____

_____

_____

_____

_____

_____

Flyer printed to raise support and funds for forty-three members of the Haganah who were arrested by the British in 1939

Israel's Declaration of Independence proclaims that the values of the State of Israel are to be based on the lessons of "liberty, justice, and peace that were taught by the Jewish prophets." Today, Israel's armed forces have an ethical code that permits soldiers to defend themselves but forbids them from needlessly injuring another person. The code requires soldiers to honor the Jewish value of the holiness of human life.

1. Do you think Israeli soldiers should be held to a higher ethical standard than other soldiers? Why or why not?

_____

_____

_____

2. List the three characteristics you think are most important for a Jewish soldier to have. Explain why each is important.

A. _____

_____

_____

B. _____

_____

_____

C. _____

_____

_____

Chapter 7

Europe Between the Wars

Rising Antisemitism and Jewish Diversity

- Why were West European Jews more assimilated into the broader secular culture than East European Jews?

- What were the different responses Jews had to antisemitism?

- How does the freedom of living in a democracy affect our Jewish identities today?

Key Words and Places

Nazi Party	Concentration Camp
Mein Kampf	Dictator
Reichstag	Nuremberg Laws

The BIG Picture

In February 1921, a group of American Jews traveled to Warsaw, Poland, bringing food, medical supplies, and money. Many of Poland's Jews lived in poverty. The Warsaw Jews welcomed the Americans, but as Boris Bogen, a member of the relief mission, recalled, "No sooner was the cheering over than they divided into many voices."

This was typical of much of European Jewry during the years after World War I. Still treated as outsiders in their home countries, Jews developed many different ideas about how to improve their living conditions. The Jewish population was diverse, including those who were Orthodox and those who were Zionists, Jews who supported revolutionary change and Jews who wanted to assimilate into the surrounding European culture.

But with each new outbreak of antisemitism, these differences mattered less and less. Blaming the Jews for the problems of Europe, Adolf Hitler rose to power in Germany in 1933. He claimed that Jews were an inferior and dangerous race that should never be permitted to assimilate into German life.

1920	1921	1925	1928
Franz Rosenzweig opens Frankfurt Free Jewish Lehrhaus to encourage Jewish education	Albert Einstein wins Nobel Prize in Physics	Adolf Hitler publishes detailed plan to seize power and rid Germany of Jews	Joseph Stalin gains power in Soviet Union

European Jewry at a Glance

Life was changing quickly in the early twentieth century. European Jews were now heavily urban. Two-thirds of Germany's Jews lived in cities of over 100,000 people, and three-quarters of Poland's Jews lived in urban areas. The 300,000 Jews of Warsaw, Poland, formed the largest Jewish community in Europe. Far more Jews now earned their living from urban industries and trade than from agriculture.

But European Jews were divided over how to respond to developments of modern science, culture, and industry. In Western Europe, where Jews had experienced emancipation and had been influenced by the Jewish Enlightenment, the modern ways of life were generally embraced. They dressed similarly to non-Jews, spoke the national language, had small families, lived in cities, and were able to move up economically to the middle class.

Some Jews became leading figures in European culture, like the founder of psycho-analysis, Sigmund Freud, Nobel Prize–winning physicist Albert Einstein, and the influential modern painter Max Beckmann. Growing numbers of Jews embraced Reform Judaism rather than traditional Orthodoxy, and more and more Jews intermarried with non-Jews.

1932

World History:
Amelia Earhart becomes first woman to fly solo across Atlantic Ocean

1933

Adolf Hitler becomes chancellor of Germany

1935

Nuremberg Laws officially strip Jews of basic rights in Germany

Albert Einstein

Albert Einstein

While many European Jews achieved great success in the early 1900's, they were not accepted as equals in most countries. The experience of Albert Einstein was typical. By the time Einstein was in his mid-twenties, he already had written a series of scientific papers that forever changed the way we understand the universe and laws of physics. Recognized as one of the world's great scientists, he was awarded a Nobel Prize in 1921.

Yet, when Adolf Hitler came to power in Germany in 1933, he ordered the burning of "subversive" books, including Einstein's work. Einstein, who was visiting the United States at the time, renounced his German citizenship and never returned. He settled in the United States and continued his research. A resident of Princeton, New Jersey, Einstein was also a human rights activist, a champion of nuclear disarmament, and a fund-raiser for the establishment of the modern State of Israel.

Einstein believed that "the life of the individual has meaning only insofar as it aids in making the life of every living thing nobler and more beautiful."

Describe one way your understanding of what it means to be a Jew helps you to add goodness to the world.

_____

_____

_____

In contrast, East European Jews faced greater legal restrictions and had less access to modern advances than West European Jews. Living in comparatively underdeveloped countries, these Jews struggled to earn a living as laborers and small-scale merchants. Some continued to live in small towns and villages. Many dressed differently from their non-Jewish neighbors, spoke Yiddish primarily, had large families, and remained Orthodox. Many also continued to observe traditional ways of life, including, in the case of men, keeping their sidelocks (*payos* in Yiddish) uncut and wearing long beards, and, in the case of married women, keeping their heads covered in public.

Soviet propaganda poster from about 1920 portrays negative view of religion

Jews in the Soviet Union

The Jews of Russia experienced one moment of hope after World War I. When the Communist Party took power in 1917, it outlawed discriminatory laws based on religion and it banned antisemitism. The government set up a special department to teach Yiddish-speaking Jews the ideals of the new Soviet Union.

It soon became clear, however, that the Communist Party's goal was not to ensure equality for Jews, but rather to stamp out Judaism in the Soviet Union. Synagogues were closed down and the publication and distribution of religious books were banned. Zionists were arrested.

Conditions for Jews worsened with Joseph Stalin's rise to power in the late 1920's. Stalin considered Jews to be outsiders and persecuted them. Jews were placed under the authority of his secret police.

However, in the years after World War I, even the most modern Jews of Europe often found themselves treated as outsiders in much of Europe. They may have considered themselves Poles, Latvians, Lithuanians, Germans, or Hungarians. But in the eyes of many of their nationalist neighbors, they were simply Jews. This would be at the heart of the coming wave of European antisemitism.

Facing the "Jewish Problem"

In the years after World War I, many Europeans spoke about Jews as a "problem." By this they meant that Jews were both different and disliked. They did not believe that Jews could ever become part of their home countries—they would forever be distinguished by religious and racial differences.

The Jews of Europe developed four different responses.

Zionists like these young Jews in Kosow, Poland, in 1922, insisted that the only place where Jews could feel at home was in their own homeland, the Land of Israel. Why do you think they believed that?

Remain Separate

Orthodox Jews believed that the Jews are a people—a nation-in-exile awaiting the Messiah, united by a shared commitment to God's law, as written in the Torah. Following the teachings of the ancient rabbis in *Pirkei Avot* ("Ethics of the Sages"), they prayed for the welfare of their nation's governments and did not call for political change. They were happy to live and work separately from non-Jews. All they asked for was the right to earn a living and practice Judaism in peace, including using Jewish law to address community issues, such as marriage and divorce.

Integrate

By contrast, integrationists insisted that Jews should differ only in religion from the people among whom they lived. In other words, they should be Poles, Germans, or French citizens of the Jewish faith. They believed that the more that Jews were similar to their non-Jewish neighbors, the more likely they were to win acceptance. For integrationists, Judaism was a religious faith only, not an ethnic or national identity.

Return to the Jewish Homeland

The Zionists agreed with the Orthodox vision of the Jews as a people, but they disagreed with the idea of attempting to live in Europe. Zionists argued that Jews needed to return to their own land, the Land of Israel, where they could speak Hebrew, develop their own culture, and govern themselves. They did not believe that Jews would ever be accepted as equals in Europe.

Support the Socialist and Communist Revolutions

Radical Jews offered a fourth idea—that the "Jewish problem" was actually part of a larger social problem that could only be solved through social revolution and the overthrow of oppressive leaders. Many of them opposed nationalism and religion, instead supporting equality and harmony among all people. Under Socialism or Communism, they believed,

You Are There

Europe

Solving the Jewish Problem

Picture yourself living in Europe after World War I. For your entire life you have heard people talking about the so-called Jewish problem. You know that Jews have developed many different responses to this problem, including remaining separate, integrating, returning to the Jewish homeland, and supporting Socialist and Communist revolutions. Which view makes the most sense to you? Or do you have your own solution? Explain the reasons behind your answer.

_____

_____

_____

economic classes and national differences would eventually disappear.

In the end, all four solutions failed to keep Jews safe as economies collapsed around the world during the Great Depression of the 1930's. Jews throughout Europe, especially in Poland and Germany, found themselves excluded from society and treated as scapegoats. In Poland, Jews were forced out of public life and barred from government jobs. Special taxes were levied against them and they were required to buy expensive work licenses. By the late 1930's, the limited number of Jews who were still being accepted to universities were made to sit apart from other students on special "ghetto benches."

Meanwhile, in Germany, economic depression forced banks and factories to close. As the Great Depression continued, increasing numbers of desperate Germans turned to a new political party—the National Socialist German Workers Party, known as the **Nazi Party.** The leader of the Nazi Party was Adolf Hitler.

The Rise of Adolf Hitler

Born in Austria in 1889, Hitler was a failed art student who lived on the fringes of society. After fighting in the German army in World War I, he expressed outrage toward those whom he believed had caused Germany to lose the war. Hitler claimed that Communists and Jews were especially to blame, and he expressed particular fury toward the Jews, whom he considered "a non-German, alien race." His

Adolf Hitler

the summer of 1933, Hitler became **dictator,** holding absolute power over the German government and people.

Living conditions for Jews in Germany immediately grew worse. New laws expelled Jews from all government positions and from many professions, including teaching. On April 1, 1933, the Nazis declared a general boycott of all Jewish shops, goods, lawyers, and doctors. Individual Jews were kidnapped, beaten, or shot. Others were thrown into one of the fifty concentration camps in Germany. On September 15, 1935, the **Nuremberg Laws** officially stripped Jews of their basic rights, including German citizenship.

But much worse lay ahead.

autobiography, ***Mein Kampf,*** meaning *My Struggle*, spelled out his plan to seize power and rid Germany of its Jews.

Promising Germans that he could erase the painful memories of their defeat in World War I and return Germany to economic prosperity, Hitler quickly built a following for his extreme right-wing party. In 1930, the Nazis received over 18 percent of the vote, entitling them to 107 of the 577 seats in the **Reichstag,** Germany's parliament. This made them the country's second-largest political party.

Hitler's followers were aggressively anti-semitic, attacking Jews on the street, disrupting Jewish religious services, and desecrating synagogues and Jewish cemeteries. The Nazis continued to gain ground, and in January 1933 Hitler was named the nation's chancellor. Using intimidation and violence, he eliminated competing political parties. He also sent many political rivals to Dachau, Germany's first **concentration camp,** or prison, for those who were considered enemies of the Nazis. By

Deprived of the freedom to study or work in their chosen fields, Jews sought to earn their livings in new ways. Charitable organizations, like the United Jewish Appeal, provided money for professional retraining and for the settlement of Jews in Palestine.

then & NOW

Following World War I, even as antisemitism grew, more and more Jews sought to explore and understand Judaism. In Germany, for example, some young Jews developed a new interest in Jewish spirituality and mysticism. Franz Rosenzweig, a philosopher who had once considered converting to Christianity, opened the Frankfurt Free Jewish Lehrhaus, meaning "house of learning." Jewish libraries and adult education programs multiplied throughout Germany.

In Poland, Jewish literature, theater, rabbinic scholarship, and dozens of Jewish newspapers flourished in Yiddish, Hebrew, and Polish. To increase popular knowledge of the Talmud, Rabbi Meir Shapira began a program for Polish Jews to study an identical page of the Talmud each day. To this day, Jews around the world follow this program, called *daf yomi* in Hebrew.

1. Why might so many Jews have become interested in learning about Judaism at a time of rising antisemitism?

_____

_____

_____

2. Today, living in democracies, not only do we have the freedom to explore Judaism but also to let go of our Jewish identities. Suggest one way to increase Jews' interest in and commitment to Judaism.

_____

_____

_____

_____

Chapter **8** The Holocaust

The Monstrous Cost of Intolerance and Indifference

investigate

- How did Hitler carry out his plan to eliminate the Jews of Europe?

- What was the response of Jews in Europe and around the world?

- How did Hitler's "final solution" change world Jewry forever?

- What lessons can we learn from the Holocaust?

Key Words and Places

Kristallnacht	Righteous Gentiles
Holocaust	Final Solution
Axis Powers	Extermination Camps
Allied Powers	Warsaw Ghetto Uprising
Babi Yar	

The **BIG** Picture

From the moment he took power in Germany, Adolf Hitler made the rebuilding of the German military a top priority. Hitler quickly constructed one of the most powerful war machines the world had ever seen and began building an empire. With each new conquest, a larger percentage of Europe's Jews fell under his control. First, in 1938, Germany annexed the neighboring country of Austria with its 200,000 Jews. Then, by 1939, it had seized Czechoslovakia, home to 357,000 Jews.

World War II began on September 1, 1939, when German forces struck east into Poland, home of Europe's largest Jewish community—more that 3.3 million Jews. In 1940 Hitler conquered Denmark, Norway, Holland, Belgium, and France. The next year he drove deep into the Soviet Union. By the end of 1941, Hitler controlled the fate of nearly 9 million Jews. He had vowed "to settle the Jewish problem." Now it was within his power to fulfill this chilling promise.

1938	1939	1940	1941	1942
Kristallnacht attacks against Jews take place throughout Germany	World War II begins	Nazis establish Warsaw ghetto	Massacre of 33,000 Jews in Babi Yar; U.S. enters World War II after Japan bombs Pearl Harbor	Wannsee Conference in Berlin; Nazi leaders devise plan to murder all European Jews

The Night of Broken Glass

On November 9, 1938, at 7 a.m. in Cologne, Germany, Ann Schwarz was awakened by screams. Hearing someone shout, "The synagogue is burning," she quickly rose and went outside. Nazi storm troopers were smashing the windows of her family's bakery. Shattered glass was flying everywhere, and the storm troopers completely destroyed the store. Ann went to the police station and was told, "Go home. We can't help you."

This government-supported pogrom known as **Kristallnacht,** "the night of shattered glass," was one of many similar attacks against Jews throughout Germany at precisely the same time. Synagogues and homes were destroyed, stores looted, and thousands of Jewish men were rounded up and taken off to concentration camps.

Those Jews who could do so, immediately left Germany. They sought refuge elsewhere in Europe, Palestine, or the United States. Some, who did not get far enough away, would meet up with Hitler again as he conquered neighboring countries and began the **Holocaust,** his deadly international campaign against the Jews.

1943

1944

1945

Warsaw Ghetto
Uprising begins

World History:
Harvard Mark I computer, first large-scale automatic digital computer in U.S., invented by Howard Aiken and programmed by Grace Hopper (inventor of COBOL)

U.S. B-29 bomber, the *Enola Gay,* drops atomic bomb on Hiroshima, Japan; Germany surrenders to Allies; World War II ends

World War II

Before World War II began in 1939, Germany and the Soviet Union had made an agreement not to go to war against each other. Hitler had no intention of keeping this pact with Stalin, the Soviet leader. He simply wanted to defeat other European armies before worrying about war with the Soviets. The German military quickly conquered most of Europe in 1939 and 1940. By early 1941 Great Britain stood alone against Hitler. Then, in June 1941, Hitler broke his pact with Stalin and attacked the Soviet Union.

Hitler had already joined forces with Italy and Japan, forming the **Axis Powers.** After Japan attacked the United States at Pearl Harbor in December 1941, the United States entered the war. Hitler now faced three great foes at once—Great Britain, the Soviet Union, and the United States, known together as the **Allied Powers.** But the Allied forces were not yet in a strong enough position to attack Nazi-controlled Europe: Hitler ruled the continent, allowing him to carry out his plan to eliminate the Jews of Europe.

As soon as the war began, the Nazis moved rapidly and methodically against the Jews. First, they evicted Jews from their homes, taking most of their belongings from them. Then, in an effort to isolate them, they packed many Jews into overcrowded ghettos in cities. Other Jews were forced into concentration camps that were quickly built all over German-held Eastern Europe. Jews healthy enough to work

Jews were rounded up and marched through the streets as bystanders looked on.

were used as slave labor for German war industries. Others were beaten, starved to death, or simply shot.

Jews were not the only victims of the Germans: Romani people (often referred to as gypsies), homosexuals, Communists, and anyone considered an opponent of the state also were targeted. The Jews, however, were attacked with special ferocity. Even non-Jewish descendants of Jews were considered to be Jews by "race" and were persecuted.

Special mobile killing forces traveled behind the German army as it stormed into the Soviet Union. When the Germans conquered an area, these forces gathered all the Jews and murdered them. Sometimes they used gas vans to kill their victims; more commonly they collected Jewish populations of entire towns, drove them into the woods, had them dig their own graves, and shot them dead on the spot. In a period of less than forty-eight hours in **Babi Yar,** northwest of Kiev, thirty-three thousand Jews were robbed of all valuables, stripped, lined up by a ravine, and shot, their lifeless bodies falling into the pit.

Historians estimate that by the end of 1941, the Nazis had worked to death, starved, shot, or

With each new German conquest, more and more Jews were caught under the Nazi heel with fewer options for escape.

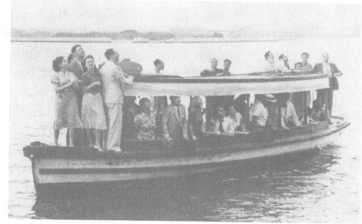

In 1939, more than 950 Jewish refugees left Germany on the ocean liner *St. Louis*, hoping to find a safe haven from Nazi persecution. But they were turned away from Cuba, the United States, and Canada, and forced to return to Europe. Many of them eventually died in Nazi concentration camps. Here we see Jews already living in Cuba helplessly watching as friends and family depart on the *St. Louis*.

gassed about one million Jews. But even this was not fast enough for Hitler.

Dreams of Escape

Jews throughout Europe sought escape—to America, to Palestine, to any place that would take them. Thousands of Jews did manage to escape, but far more were trapped. Most of the nations of the world, including the United States and Canada, had quotas on the number of Jews permitted to enter their countries.

With antisemitism rising and the American economy suffering, two-thirds of Americans in 1938 believed that Jewish refugees should be kept out of the country. Even a bill to admit twenty thousand refugee children was defeated. When asked how many Jews should be admitted to Canada, Frederick Charles Blair, the director of the Immigration Branch of the Canadian Department of Mines and Resources, responded, "None is too many."

Other countries were no better. England refused to admit Jewish refugees into Palestine. Latin American nations admitted some, but then closed their doors. Cuba actually revoked the entry permits of many Jews already in Cuba.

73

Anne Frank

Anne Frank

Anne Frank was born in Germany in 1929. Her family fled to Holland to escape the Nazis when she was four years old. But the Nazis took control of Holland in 1940 and began sending Dutch Jews to concentration camps by 1942. Forced into hiding, Anne's family found refuge in a secret set of rooms in an office building in Amsterdam. There they lived with several other Jews—Fritz Pfeffer and the Van Pels family—until August 4, 1944, when the police discovered them and sent them to a concentration camp. Anne died less than a year later, at age fifteen.

Anne kept a diary from June 12, 1942, to August 1, 1944. She decided that after the war she would publish a book based on her diary. Anne did not live to fulfill her dream or to write other books that might also have enriched the world. However, her father, Otto Frank, did survive the war and published her diary.

On Thursday, July 6, 1944, Anne wrote: "We're all alive, but we don't know why or what for; we're all searching for happiness; we're all leading lives that are different and yet the same.... Earning happiness means doing good and working."

What lessons might you learn from Anne's words?

_____

_____

_____

Describe an action that Anne's words inspire you to take.

_____

_____

Righteous Gentiles

Amid the terror and tragedy of the Holocaust, or *Shoah,* there were heroic non-Jews, known as "Righteous Gentiles," who showed great courage and humanity by risking their own lives to save Jewish lives. In Budapest, Hungary, a Swedish diplomat named Raoul Wallenberg printed and issued Swedish citizenship papers to thousands of Hungarian Jews. Sweden was neutral in the war, making Swedish citizens off-limits to Nazi forces. Wallenberg also set up "Swedish houses"—buildings flying the Swedish flag, where Jews could live in safety. His actions saved thousands of Hungarian Jews.

Similarly, tens of thousands of Jewish children, known as "hidden children," were saved by Righteous Gentiles. They were hidden in places such as convents, or "adopted" by Christian families who pretended that they were their own children.

Name one character trait of a Righteous Gentile. Explain why you think so.

_____

_____

The Final Solution

When Hitler saw that no country would accept masses of Jewish refugees, he became even bolder in his plans. By 1942 Hitler and other high-level Nazi officials were discussing what they called a **"final solution"** to their Jewish problem, a plan to murder all European Jews.

Within months, the Nazis built a series of **extermination camps,** or death camps, in places such as Sobibor, Treblinka, and Auschwitz. They were designed as factories of mass murder. Railroad tracks ran right up to the camp entrances. Huge gas chambers were built, enabling camp officials to murder hundreds of Jews at once using poison gas.

The Germans preferred to use the extermination camps to kill Jews: it was more efficient. Most of the Jews of Greece—Sephardic Jews— were deported to Auschwitz in the spring of 1943 and killed. A year later, some 437,000 Jews from Hungary were sent to Auschwitz in just two months. Most of them were murdered, too.

Jews arriving in Auschwitz with their few belongings

The War Against
the Jews

- ◎ Concentration camps
- ◙ Extermination camps
- ● Large-scale massacres
- ● Large ghettos

Before the Holocaust, more than 9 million Jews lived in Europe. By the end of the Holocaust, only 3 million had survived.

The Warsaw Ghetto Uprising and Other Resistance

Although practically powerless in the face of the German war machine, there were Jews who tried to resist. For some, this meant struggling to survive in the camps. For others, it meant spiritual resistance: practicing Judaism in the face of the Nazi threat. For still others, resistance meant taking up arms. Beginning in 1942, as Jews learned more about Nazi death camps, some escaped to the forest to fight in the underground movement. Others gathered weapons within Jewish ghettos, determined to fight to the death.

In Warsaw, a German effort to send Jews from the ghetto to concentration camps on the eve of Passover 1943 met with massive resistance. Most of the resisters died and the ghetto was destroyed, but the story of the Warsaw Ghetto Uprising inspired Jews and non-Jews alike.

In the concentration camp Auschwitz-Birkenau, on October 7, 1944, Jews dynamited a crematorium (furnace used to burn the bodies of inmates) and set fires. More than twenty-three other Jewish uprisings have been documented in ghettos, labor camps, and death camps.

Jewish underground fighters

The End of the War

By 1944 Germany was clearly losing the war. In June, Allied forces began driving east toward Germany. Soviet forces, meanwhile, had pushed the German army out of Soviet territory and were rolling west toward Germany. On April 30, 1945, with the Soviet army closing in on Berlin, Hitler shot and killed himself. Germany surrendered on May 7.

As the Germans retreated, they tried to destroy evidence of their crimes, blowing up gas chambers and burning documents. But they didn't have time to complete the cover-up. The first extermination camp to be liberated by the Allies was Maidanek, in Lublin, Poland, in July 1944. Over the following year, the rest of the camps were liberated.

At least six million Jews were dead: either gassed, shot, starved, beaten, left to die from

Death Toll of European Jews

◎ Poland	2,700,000	◎ Yugoslavia	51,400
◎ Soviet Union	2,100,000	◎ Austria	48,767
◎ Hungary	559,250	◎ Belgium (including people of other nationalities)	28,000
◎ Germany	144,000		
◎ Czechoslovakia	143,000	◎ Bulgaria	7,335
◎ Romania	120,919	◎ Italy	5,596
◎ Netherlands	102,000	◎ Norway	758
◎ France (including people of other nationalities)	76,000	◎ Luxembourg	720
		◎ Albania	591
◎ Greece	58,443	◎ Denmark	116

disease and exposure, or killed on death marches as Allied troops closed in on Germany late in the war.

Roughly three million European Jews survived: Some had managed to escape the continent. Others were saved by non-Jews who hid and assisted them. Still others were found alive when the death camps were finally liberated.

After the war, Europe was no longer the spiritual and population center of world Jewry; far more Jews now lived in North America. Many of the surviving European Jews left for non-European Jewish communities, such as those in the United States, Canada, and Australia. Those Jews who did return to their homes found themselves part of much smaller Jewish communities or, in fact, found nothing at all of their old homes. Yet other survivors left for Palestine, convinced that the Jewish future lay in the Land of Israel.

These Jewish refugees survived the Holocaust and the threat of postwar pogroms in Poland. Here they are gathering in the streets of Bratislava, Czechoslovakia in September 1946 as they begin their journey to Palestine. What might some of their hopes and dreams have been?

Hitler succeeded in his monstrous acts because so many everyday citizens remained silent in the face of evil. One cannot but question how many millions of lives might have been saved had more people found the courage to speak up and act.

In 1993, one of the few Jewish families in the small city of Billings, Montana, celebrated Ḥanukkah by placing a menorah in their living room window. Shortly thereafter, vandals threw a rock through the window.

A day or two later the local newspaper printed a large picture of a menorah and, with the help of local churches, encouraged all citizens of Billings to tape the image to their living room and store windows. Nearly ten thousand families and shops did so, and the vandalism stopped.

1. Why might it be easier and more effective to work as a group or community, such as a synagogue, when pursuing justice and fighting prejudice?

_____

_____

_____

_____

2. What issue do you think people should speak up about and do something about in our time? Describe why you think the issue is important and what should be done.

_____

_____

_____

_____

_____

Chapter 9

The Birth of the Modern State of Israel

Turning Our Dream into Reality

investigate

- What challenges did the Jews of Palestine face?

- How did the spirit of Jewish unity help them overcome the challenges?

- Why might Diaspora Jews feel greater pride in their Jewish identities because of the achievements of Israeli Jews?

Key Words and Places

Displaced Persons (DPs)	Operation Magic Carpet
DP Camps	Operation Ezra and Nehemiah
Exodus 1947	
Eidot Hamizrah (Mizrahi Jews)	Ma'abarot

The **BIG** Picture

People liked to say that he was the first Jewish general since Judah Maccabee. New Yorker David "Mickey" Marcus had shown little interest in Zionism until he came face-to-face with the Nazi atrocities upon visiting the Dachau concentration camp shortly after it was liberated. Marcus's interactions with the survivors convinced him that the Jews needed a homeland of their own. Three years later he was in Palestine helping to turn the underground Haganah into a disciplined, modern army, and playing a critical role in the War of Independence.

Mickey Marcus was motivated by a strong sense of Jewish unity. This same spirit gave the Jews of Palestine the power to stand up to the British and to defeat the Arabs. It motivated their concern for and responses to Jews in distress, like the lifesaving airlifts of Jews from Iraq and Yemen that the new State of Israel organized.

1946	1947		
Irgun bombs King David Hotel in Jerusalem	**World History:** Jackie Robinson plays for Brooklyn Dodgers, ending segregation in Major League Baseball	*Exodus 1947* sets sail for Palestine carrying 4,500 Jewish refugees	UN General Assembly votes to partition Palestine into Jewish and Arab states

The Surviving Remnant

Europe was in ruins. Millions of people were displaced by the war, including tens of thousands of Holocaust survivors. The Allied armies and the United Nations Relief and Rehabilitation Administration (UNNRA) provided aid for the **displaced persons (DPs),** helping to return the DPs to their countries of origin.

But many Jews refused to go home. Most of their loved ones were dead and the lives they had known before the war were shattered beyond repair. Other Jews returned to their towns and villages, only to find that they were not wanted. In Poland, antisemitism was still so strong that some Jews were brutally attacked by their former neighbors.

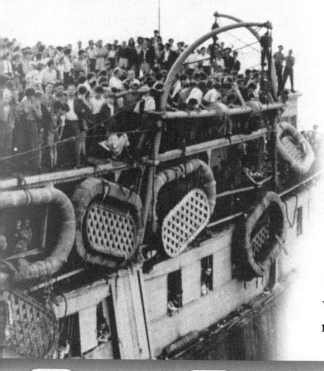

Jewish underground fighters and soldiers from the Jewish Brigade of the British army secretly helped move many of these survivors across the Polish border and through Europe to **DP camps,** or refugee camps, in Germany, Austria, and Italy. Some DP camps were located on the sites of former concentration camps like Bergen-Belsen. By 1947, the camps were teeming with 250,000 Jews. At first, there were terrible shortages of food and clothing. The UN and non-governmental organizations worked to improve conditions. The American Jewish Joint Distribution Committee provided the survivors with food, clothing, school supplies, books, and religious articles such as Bibles.

1948

Establishment of independent modern State of Israel

1949

Israel holds first election

Operation Magic Carpet begins, bringing about 47,000 Jews from Yemen to Israel

Britain and the Jewish Refugee Problem

Even after the war, the British refused to abolish the White Paper and allow DPs to go to Palestine. Dependent on Middle Eastern oil, they did not want to anger the Arabs, who opposed Jewish immigration. In order to increase pressure on the British, the Haganah brought thousands of DPs to southern Europe, where they set sail for Palestine. But in 90 percent of the cases the British stopped the ships before they reached Palestine, sending the Jews to detention camps instead.

In January 1947, hurting from severe economic problems at home and unable to effectively address the competing demands of Arabs and Jews, Britain handed the problem in Palestine over to the United Nations. A UN Special Committee on Palestine (UNSCOP)

Holocaust survivors in a DP camp study Hebrew in preparation for resettling in Palestine

Underground Resistance

The Jewish underground militias in Palestine also used force to pressure Britain into changing its policies. For eighteen months the Haganah, Irgun, and the more radical Lohamei Heirut Israel (Lehi) sabotaged railway tracks and attacked police posts, airfields, and radar installations. The British sent eighty thousand troops to Palestine to put down the violence and round up the attackers.

Cooperation among the Jewish militias fell apart after the bombing of the British military and civilian headquarters in Jerusalem's King David Hotel. The explosion occurred on July 22, 1946, and killed about ninety people—British, Arabs, and Jews. Its mastermind, Irgun leader Menahem Begin, claimed that warnings of the attack had been given.

The attacks and British retaliations continued. But the hotel bombing soured much of the *Yishuv* on the use of terror. *Yishuv* leaders did not want an all-out war with the British. They even urged parents to turn in their own children if the children joined Irgun or Lehi.

was created. Made up of representatives from eleven neutral countries, its job was to investigate the situation and report back to the UN General Assembly.

Exodus 1947

Meanwhile, the Haganah continued its efforts to bring refugees to Palestine. *Exodus 1947*, a former American passenger ship that the Haganah had acquired and renamed, set sail for Palestine from France in July 1947 with close to 4,500 Jewish refugees aboard, including 655 children. As the ship neared Palestine, British destroyers rammed and boarded it. The passengers tried to defend themselves and a short battle followed—two refugees and one crewman died, and thirty people were injured.

The British towed the ship to Haifa's harbor, forced the refugees onto British navy transports, and sent them back to Europe. When the transports arrived in France, the passengers refused to get off and declared a hunger strike. But the British sent them back to the DP camps in Germany.

Passengers on *Exodus 1947*. A year after being turned back to the DP camps in Germany, more than half of the *Exodus 1947* passengers attempted *aliyah* again and were successful. The remaining passengers settled in Israel after the establishment of the country in 1948.

UNSCOP members, who were in Haifa during a fact-finding mission, witnessed the events with horror. Newspapers gave the story front-page coverage, calling the *Exodus 1947* a "floating Auschwitz." The incident helped sway world opinion in favor of the Zionists.

The UN Partition Plan

The UNSCOP committee presented its report in August 1947. It recommended that the British mandate end. A majority of the committee members supported the partitioning of Palestine—its division into two separate states, one Jewish, the other Arab—with Jerusalem under international authority.

The Arabs were outraged and threatened war. They outnumbered Jews two to one in Palestine, yet received only about 45 percent of the territory. Why, they complained, should Arabs pay the price for Europe's persecution of the Jews? The Jews, who felt that they had been promised a much larger territory under the Balfour Declaration, nevertheless accepted the partition plan, which promised Jews self-rule and unlimited immigration.

On November 29, 1947, the UN General Assembly voted on the partition plan. The final vote was 33 in favor, 13 against, with 10 abstentions. The British announced that they would leave Palestine in May 1948.

As crowds of Jews celebrated the news in Jerusalem's streets, they were addressed by an overjoyed leader of the *Yishuv*, Golda Myerson. "For two thousand years we have waited for our deliverance," she declared. "Now that it is here it is so great and so wonderful that it surpasses

Fighting for Control of Palestine

Between December 1947 and May 1948, as the British looked on, hostilities raged between the Zionists and the Arabs for control of Palestine. In the early months of the fighting the Jews were on the defensive. The road between Tel Aviv and Jerusalem was cut off and the Jewish community within Jerusalem was under fire. In April, an arms shipment from Czechoslovakia helped the Haganah gain the offensive. By early May, it captured Haifa, Jaffa, and most of the Galilee.

Meanwhile, Arab militias and the Irgun and Leḥi engaged in a tit-for-tat terror campaign. Houses, buses, office buildings, oil refineries, and hotels were bombed and ambushed. Hundreds of Jewish and Arab civilians were killed.

In mid-April, Irgun and Leḥi fighters attacked the Arab village of Deir Yassin, along the Tel Aviv–Jerusalem road, killing scores of civilians. Hearing of the violence, many Arabs in surrounding areas fled. Days after the Deir Yassin attack, Arab militiamen ambushed a ten-vehicle convoy of Jewish doctors and nurses headed for Hadassah hospital, murdering more than seventy Jews.

human words. Jews, *mazal tov!*" David Ben-Gurion was less joyous. He later recalled, "I looked at them so happy dancing, but I could only think that they were all going to war."

Israel's War of Independence

Finally, on the morning of May 14, 1948, the British lowered their flag from the Government House in Jerusalem. At 4:00 p.m., Jewish leaders gathered in the Tel Aviv Museum under a portrait of Theodor Herzl. Ben-Gurion banged his gavel to bring the gathering to order and the crowd spontaneously began singing Hatikvah. Then Ben-Gurion read the Scroll of Independence, proclaiming, "We, members of the People's Council, representatives of the Jewish community of *Eretz Yisrael* and of the Zionist movement…hereby proclaim the establishment of a Jewish State in *Eretz Yisrael*, to be called the State of Israel."

But there was little time for celebration. Before dawn the next day, four Egyptian fighter planes attacked Tel Aviv. Arab armies from neighboring countries launched an invasion on three fronts, but by early June the Israelis gained strength, stopping the Egyptian advance in the south and repelling attacks from the Syrians and Iraqis in the northeast.

Israel made important gains in the later stages of the war, capturing the Negev in the south and widening the narrow corridor of land between Jerusalem and Tel Aviv. By the time the fighting ended, Israel controlled 80 percent of Palestine. Jordan controlled the West Bank and East Jerusalem, including the Old City, and Egypt controlled the Gaza Strip.

Golda (Myerson) Meir

Golda Meir

Golda Mabovitch was born in Kiev, Ukraine, in 1898, immigrated to the United States with her family, and became a schoolteacher and passionate Zionist. In 1921, she and her husband, Morris Myerson, settled on Kibbutz Merḥavyah in Palestine.

Golda Myerson quickly became active in Zionist politics. Among her many contributions, she conducted secret negotiations with Jordan's King Abdullah that helped limit Jordan's involvement in Israel's War of Independence. In 1956, at Prime Minister Ben-Gurion's request, she changed her name from Myerson to Meir, a Hebrew name. She was foreign minister of Israel from 1956 to 1965, and she became Israel's fourth prime minister in 1969. She died in 1978.

Meir was one of only two women to sign Israel's Declaration of Independence. She later recalled: "After I signed, I cried. When I studied American history as a schoolgirl and I read about those who signed the Declaration of Independence, I couldn't imagine these were real people doing something real. And there I was…signing a declaration of independence."

If you could participate in one important event in Jewish history, what would you want it to be? Why?

_____

_____

_____

Casualties were heavy on both sides, although there was no doubt that Israel had won the war and gained its independence. There were early signs that the Arab states might be ready to negotiate permanent peace treaties with Israel. But the Israelis considered Arab demands for territory to be too high. "The neighboring states do not deserve an inch of Israel's land," insisted Ben-Gurion. "We are ready for peace in exchange for peace." In the end, no peace treaties were signed.

On January 25, 1949, Israel held its first election. Ben-Gurion's Labor Party won the most seats and formed the first government with Ben-Gurion as prime minister.

The Palestinian Refugees

What Israel calls the War of Independence is known in Palestinian history as the *Naqba*, or "Catastrophe." Over 700,000 Arabs fled or were forced from their homes in the territory that became the State of Israel. When the war was over, the Israeli government did not allow them to return. The Israelis feared that the Arabs would not support the Jewish State and might eventually become the majority, which would pose a threat to the Jewish character of Israel. Many Palestinian refugees never gave up the hope of returning to their former homes.

The 150,000 Arabs who remained in Israel, meanwhile, were officially granted equal rights under Israel's Declaration of Independence. But in practice, the government was suspicious of their loyalties. Military rule was declared over many Arab towns and villages near Israel's borders and

Israel Survives

The U.N. partition plan:
- Jewish territory
- Arab territory
- Territory under international authority
— Israel's borders after the War of Independence

LEBANON

SYRIA

Mediterranean Sea

Haifa

Sea of Galilee

Tel Aviv

Jericho

Jerusalem

Gaza

Dead Sea

ISRAEL

JORDAN

NEGEV DESERT

EGYPT

N
W E
S

0   30 MI
0   30 KM

Gulf of Aqaba

SAUDI ARABIA

As a result of Israel's War of Independence, its borders were actually expanded.

was only lifted in 1966. Studies indicate that discrimination against Arab communities and individuals continues to this day.

A Flood of Newcomers

With the hostilities over, chief among Israel's challenges was absorbing the waves of immigrants pouring into the country from Europe and the Middle East. They came by boat, by airplane, and even on foot. Between 1948 and 1951, almost 700,000 Jews arrived in Israel, more than doubling the size of its Jewish population.

Half of the newcomers were European Holocaust survivors, including 136,000 DPs. (Another 115,000 survivors immigrated to Western countries including the United States, Canada, and South Africa.) The other half moving to Israel arrived from Middle Eastern and North African countries—some of the oldest Jewish communities in the world. These Jews are referred to as **Eidot Hamizrah,** or **Mizrahi** Jews.

Conditions for Jews in many Arab countries deteriorated after the creation of the State of Israel. Many Mizrahi Jews left their homes eager to start new lives in Israel and Western countries like France, the United States, and Canada. But others, especially in North Africa, were attached to their homes and cultures and less willing to leave. Continued Arab-Israeli tension, particularly in the 1960's, eventually forced most of them to evacuate. By 1974, about 600,000 Mizrahi refugees had settled in Israel.

In a secret airlift called **Operation Magic Carpet,** about 47,000 Jews from Yemen were brought to Israel. Many walked hundreds of miles across rugged terrain to the British colony of Aden, where the Joint Distribution Committee cared for them until American planes could fly them to safety. Between 1950 and 1952, 110,000 Jews were evacuated to Israel from Iraq in **Operation Ezra and Nehemiah.** Tens of thousands also arrived from Morocco and Libya.

Helping these immigrants learn Hebrew, find homes, and earn a living was a huge task. Half were between the ages of fifteen and forty-five, and able to enter the army or the workforce. Only 50 percent of those were skilled in a trade or profession and only 16 percent had a high school or higher education.

Housing, in particular, was a major problem. Immigrants were arriving faster than homes could be built. Many of the earliest immigrants, mostly survivors from Europe, moved into

Palestinians as Pawns

Using the Palestinian Arab refugees as pawns in a political game served the purposes of both the Arab and Israeli governments. Arab governments, with the exception of Jordan, refused to accept the refugees as citizens of their own countries. They wanted the refugee problem to be a thorn in the side of Israel. So they kept the Palestinians in refugee camps along their border with Israel, where the Palestinians' anger and frustration toward Israel would grow and their plight would be on display for the whole world to see.

Israel, for its part, wanted to pressure the Arabs to negotiate a peace treaty. So it refused to compensate the Palestinians until a more comprehensive agreement could be worked out.

Most passengers on Operation Magic Carpet had never even seen a plane before, let alone flown in one.

A tent camp in 1953

The Challenges of Diversity

Many long-established Israelis looked down on Mizraḥi Jews, showing little respect for their traditions. Government policies encouraged Mizraḥi Jews to assimilate into Israeli society and shed their cultural distinctiveness. This created much anger and resentment among the immigrants.

One government official warned in 1949 that the Mizraḥi immigrants were becoming "a kind of second nation." As time went on, the second-class status of the Mizraḥi Jews became set. In general, they were more poorly educated, held lower-paying jobs, and were overrepresented in prisons and underrepresented in government.

In Israel, as in the United States and other democracies, it is a continuing challenge to offer equal opportunity and to balance national unity with respect for diversity.

houses vacated by the fleeing Arabs. When this supply was exhausted, many were forced to live temporarily in tent camps and *ma'abarot,* makeshift shantytowns.

Looking to the Future

By the early 1950's, major problems that continue to confront Israel today were already clear—in particular, social inequality, the status of Israeli Arabs, the conflict with Arab neighbors, and the problem of Palestinian refugees. But the founders of the modern State of Israel also had many achievements. After two thousand years, they reestablished an independent Jewish state. Moreover, in just three and a half years Israel doubled its population and turned peoples from many nations with diverse cultures, languages, and views into one people working toward a common future.

Israel's concern for abandoned people extends beyond the needs of Jews. When the boat people of Southeast Asia were drowning at sea in the 1970's, Israel opened its borders to them. Following the catastrophic nuclear accident at Chernobyl in 1986, Israeli experts flew to the Soviet Union to help save hundreds of lives. And, in 1999, when Turkey suffered an earthquake that killed and injured thousands of people, Israel sent a two-hundred-member team and a field hospital to help in the rescue effort.

Of course, like other countries, Israel has not always lived up to its ideals. In the past, many Arab communities in Israel lacked bomb shelters and early warning systems to help them survive rocket attacks. In addition, there have been numerous instances when foreign workers were unjustly deprived of their rights.

1. Do Israel's acts of compassion affect how you feel about being a Jew and how you feel about Israel? Why or why not?

_____

_____

_____

_____

2. The prophet Isaiah taught that Israel must be a light unto the nations by modeling just and compassionate behavior for others. Do you think that it is realistic or fair to hold Israel or other democratic countries to this standard? Why or why not?

_____

_____

_____

Chapter 10 "Making It" in America, 1945–1965
U.S. Jewry's "Golden Decades"

investigate

- What were the signs that Jews were more accepted in the United States after World War II than before the war?

- How did participation in synagogue life and in political and social activism reinforce for Jews both their American *and* Jewish identities?

- What can we learn from these experiences?

Key Words

McCarthyism   Prophetic Judaism

Blacklists

The BIG Picture

Baseball has long been a symbol of American culture. So it makes sense that American Jews swelled with pride as they cheered for Hank Greenberg, baseball's first Jewish superstar. Greenberg's success in the 1930's and 1940's became a symbol of the Jews' success in America.

The child of immigrants, Greenberg never tried to hide his Jewish identity by changing his name. In fact, he wore it as a badge of honor. "I just had to show [the non-Jews] that a Jew could play ball," Greenberg once explained. "I came to feel that if I, as a Jew, hit a home run, I was hitting one against Hitler."

That a Jew could master America's favorite pastime seemed to prove that Jews were no longer outsiders. Indeed, the years between 1945 and 1965 are sometimes referred to as the Golden Decades in American Jewish history. Jews joined synagogues in record numbers and became political and civil rights activists as expressions of both their American and their Jewish identities.

1947	1950	1951	1954
William Levitt begins building suburban community of Levittown, NY; Ramah summer camps opened	Julius and Ethel Rosenberg arrested on charges of spying for Soviet Union	O.S.R.U.I., first Reform summer camp in U.S., founded	300th anniversary of settlement of Jews in U.S.

Postwar Opportunities

Americans were eager to make a fresh start after World War II. Returning soldiers were especially eager to settle down and put their energies into work and family. In 1944, Congress created a program called the G.I. Bill to help soldiers pay for college and buy homes. Thousands of Jewish veterans who could not have afforded college before the war now could. At the same time, many universities were ending their quotas that limited Jewish enrollment.

Young families were becoming eager to move out of the inner cities and into the suburbs. More affordable automobiles and the growing network of highways helped make this dream possible. William Levitt, a Jewish builder from Brooklyn, recognized the growing demand for inexpensive suburban housing. Levitt had used the techniques of mass production to build army bases during the war. Now he quickly built inexpensive homes on Long Island, on the outskirts of New York City. Soon his technique spread and suburban communities mushroomed around urban centers throughout North America.

By 1948, there were enough Jews in Levittown, Long Island, to support a synagogue. The popularity of the suburban lifestyle continued to grow, and by 1965, one-third of the American Jewish community had relocated to suburban communities around the country.

1957

World History:
Space satellite,
Sputnik I, launched
by Soviet Union

1963

President John
F. Kennedy
assassinated

1964

Two Jewish civil
rights workers mur-
dered by Ku Klux
Klan in Mississippi

1965

One-third of the
American Jewish
community now
lives in suburbs

Growing interest in the American-Jewish consumer is seen in this 1940's Yiddish advertising brochure for Tide laundry detergent.

Antisemitism on the Decline

Antisemitism, which peaked just before and during World War II, greatly declined in the late 1940's and into the 1950's. Nazism had made antisemitism seem less respectable to most people. Military service also softened prejudices. Americans who had never been exposed to Jews before fought side by side with them. They learned that Jews were good, loyal fighters and that their similarities with Jews outweighed religious or ethnic differences. Finally, as economic conditions improved, people were less likely to seek scapegoats for their financial problems.

Heading South

Postwar Americans were moving by the thousands to the Sunbelt. Cities like Los Angeles and Miami were magnets for Jews. Many Jewish G.I.s from the north had done their basic military training in the Sunbelt and had fallen in love with the climate and, sometimes, with a young person from the area.

By 1960 there were almost 400,000 Jews living in Los Angeles, and close to 200,000 in Miami. Miami was especially attractive to senior citizens from the Northeast eager to escape the icy winter months. Cheaper air travel and the invention of air-conditioning helped speed up the move to the South.

Homerun king Hank Greenberg served in China during World War II. In 1954, he became the first Jewish player to be elected to baseball's Hall of Fame in Cooperstown, New York.

New York City Mayor Fiorello LaGuardia (center, holding hat) at a pro-tolerance rally in about 1944

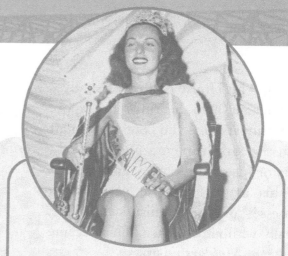

A Jewish Miss America

A symbol of the new atmosphere of acceptance was the crowning of Bess Myerson as Miss America in September 1945. Before Myerson, no Jew had ever won the Miss America beauty pageant. American Jews were thrilled.

Until this time, the definition of beauty had suggested a blue-eyed blonde with straight hair. Now it had expanded to include Myerson's dark eyes and wavy brown hair. It was as if America was once and for all rejecting old antisemitic stereotypes.

By the 1950's American Jews were receiving widespread acceptance. Judaism had become acknowledged as America's third great faith, alongside Protestantism and Catholicism. American leaders began to routinely speak of the country's Judeo-Christian values, rather than Christian values. And television stations began wishing their viewers not only a Merry Christmas but also a Happy Ḥanukkah.

Jews and McCarthyism

While the increased acceptance helped American Jews feel more secure than ever, many continued to believe that their situation could become unstable. They feared that any negative information about the Jewish community could trigger a backlash from the general American public.

Some were concerned that such a backlash could result from the rising fear of Communism that swept the United States in the late 1940's into the 1950's. Tensions between the United States and the Soviet Union were high and many Americans worried that Communists might secretly be weakening America from within. The House of Representatives and Senate held hearings to expose Communists in the entertainment industry, government, and military. Senator Joseph McCarthy gained fame for his aggressive style of accusing witnesses of Communist sympathies, usually without evidence. This became known as **McCarthyism.**

Jews were particularly concerned because many Jews had been Socialists or Communists before World War II. Many broke with Communism after Stalin's 1939 alliance with Hitler. Still others abandoned their Communist beliefs when they learned about Stalin's violent persecution of Jews. But some Jews remained committed Communists or Socialists. Now Jewish groups had to deal with such members of the community and their impact on the public's view of Jews as a whole.

Many American Jewish organizations responded to the fear and hysteria by firing employees who were known or even suspected Communists. Some Jewish community centers were directed by other Jewish organizations not to invite Communists as speakers. In Hollywood, movie studios run by Jews as well as those run by non-Jews refused to hire people whose names appeared on **blacklists,** lists of writers and actors suspected of having Communist ties.

The Rosenberg Case

In August 1949, the Soviet Union tested its first atomic bomb. Shocked that Soviet scientists had developed the bomb so quickly, the U.S. government suspected that they must have received secret information from spies in America. The following year, Julius and Ethel Rosenberg were arrested on charges of spying for the Soviet Union.

The Rosenbergs proclaimed their innocence, and left-wing groups insisted that the charges against them were motivated by antisemitism. Yet Jewish leaders who believed the Rosenbergs might be innocent most often refused to publicly defend them, even after both were tried and sentenced to death.

The Rosenbergs' guilt or innocence has been debated ever since. Today, newly discovered documents have persuaded most historians that Julius Rosenberg did pass atomic secrets to the Russians. Ethel played, at most, a supportive role in the affair. The Rosenbergs were the only convicted spies to be executed during this period.

Demonstrators protesting the death sentence for convicted spies Julius and Ethel Rosenberg

The careers and lives of many Jews (and non-Jews) were ruined by the time McCarthyism ended in the mid-1950's. But McCarthyism never developed into an antisemitic movement. And over the next thirty years, antisemitism in the United States continued to decline.

Remaking Judaism

If a fear of Communism was characteristic of postwar America, so, too, was a religious revival. Christian Americans were flocking to churches in greater numbers than during the Depression and World War II. American Jews also participated in the religious revival, joining synagogues and sending their children to religious schools in record numbers.

Increased prosperity and the move to suburbia helped fuel the greatest synagogue building boom in American Jewish history. Over a thousand synagogues were built between 1945 and 1965. They included not only sanctuaries for prayers, but also religious school classrooms, social halls, and sometimes even recreational facilities, such as gyms and swimming pools.

The Conservative movement was growing especially rapidly and soon became the largest movement within American Judaism. While maintaining a great deal of traditional observance, it also introduced new approaches and practices. In 1950, for example, its law committee voted to allow Jews to drive to synagogue and to use electricity on Shabbat. While angering some traditionalists, these innovations appealed to many second- and third-generation Jews who

The New Synagogues: Social or Sacred Centers?

Most of the new synagogue centers were part of the Conservative and Reform movements. Suburban Jews looked to the synagogue as a substitute for the urban ethnic communities they had left behind.

For many members, the social, recreational, and educational components of the synagogue center were far more central to their daily lives than the sanctuary. Synagogue attendance rates were much lower among Jews than church attendance among Christians.

wanted a modernized Judaism but also wanted to keep their ties to the practices of their youth.

The Reform movement was also growing and evolving. In the years before World War II the movement had begun to take on more of a Jewish community identity. It embraced Zionism, for example, and revived some of the religious rituals it had abandoned earlier. By the late 1950's into the 1960's, many Reform rabbis energized their congregants by emphasizing **prophetic Judaism,** or the ethical teachings of the Hebrew prophets. They particularly provided leadership on issues of social justice, such as civil rights and the fight against discrimination.

Abraham Joshua Heschel

Many rabbis were involved in the civil rights struggle. Among them was a leading Jewish thinker, Abraham Joshua Heschel. Born into a distinguished Ḥasidic family in Warsaw, Poland, in 1907, Heschel was trained as an Orthodox rabbi. In 1937, he also received a doctorate in philosophy in Berlin.

Abraham Heschel and his wife, Sylvia, with Pope Paul VI in 1964

Heschel was deported to Poland by the Nazis in 1938. He went to England and then to America where, from 1940 to 1945, he taught at the Reform rabbinical seminary in Cincinnati. He then taught at the Conservative seminary in New York City from 1945 to his death in 1972.

In March 1965, Heschel joined Martin Luther King, Jr. in a voting rights protest march in Selma, Alabama. "I felt as though my legs were praying," Heschel wrote. A refugee from Nazism, he strongly believed that Judaism demands active participation in advancing social justice. "The opposite of good is not evil," Heschel wrote. "The opposite of good is indifference."

Why do you think Rabbi Heschel compared marching for civil rights to praying?

_____

_____

What is the lesson of Rabbi Heschel's statement: "The opposite of good is indifference"? Do you agree or disagree? Why?

_____

_____

_____

Jews Become Activists

Thousands of Jews in the 1950's and 1960's, including many college students, participated in the struggle on behalf of civil rights for African-Americans. Jews took part in sit-in protests, freedom rides, and protest marches. In 1958, The Temple in Atlanta, Georgia, was bombed because its rabbi, Jacob Rothschild, was a passionate supporter of equality for all Atlanta's citizens. For many Jews and non-Jews, the bombing was a wake-up call, a reminder that anyone who dared speak out against social injustice could become a target of hatred.

In the summer of 1964, almost two-thirds of the white volunteers who participated in a black voter registration drive in Mississippi were Jews. Two of these Jewish civil rights workers, Andrew Goodman and Michael Schwerner, were murdered by Ku Klux Klan members, along with a black colleague, James Earl Chaney.

Not all American Jews were happy about the high-profile involvement of Jews in the civil rights movement. Many southern Jews resented the northern Jewish civil rights workers. Indeed, the involvement of northern Jews in desegregation efforts sparked a

Lessons of the Holocaust

Emil Fackenheim, a Holocaust survivor, philosopher, and Reform rabbi, voiced the concern that American Jews were raising children who valued only secular issues of social justice. He believed they had no appreciation for the traditional Jewish rituals and ceremonies that distinguished and separated Jews from their neighbors; no appreciation for the beauty of Shabbat; no interest in serious Jewish education; in short, no desire to ensure the survival of the Jewish people.

For Fackenheim, the lesson of the Holocaust was that Jews needed to worry first and foremost about themselves. He taught that Jews must add a 614th mitzvah to the traditional 613: Thou shalt not assimilate—do not abandon your Jewish identity. Fackenheim believed that shedding one's Judaism was like granting Hitler victory after his death.

Heschel saw the lesson of the Holocaust in broader terms. As a victim of Nazism, he felt that Jews must never be silent again when confronted with the persecution of any group of people.

Both rabbis were committed to the teachings of prophetic Judaism and both were concerned about the survival of Judaism and the Jews, but each used the memory of the Holocaust to stress a different lesson.

In your own words, describe the lesson Fackenheim stressed. Then describe the lesson Heschel stressed.

Fackenheim _____

_____

_____

Heschel _____

_____

_____

wave of antisemitism directed against southern Jews. Some Jewish-owned businesses were boycotted and synagogues firebombed.

As the 1960's continued, American Jews also helped lead other movements in the pursuit of justice. They demanded the right to free speech on college campuses, protested America's war in Vietnam, and rallied for women's rights. Many were inspired by the prophetic Judaism promoted by liberal rabbis. Sacred teachings, such as "Let justice well up as waters and righteousness as a mighty stream" (Amos 5:24), strengthened both their commitment to Judaism and to their pursuit of justice as Americans.

Other American Jews felt alienated from Judaism. They associated it with the suburban lifestyle of their parents, which they saw as spiritually empty and materialistic.

The Price of Success?

American Jews had "made it" in America. Antisemitism was on the decline and the lifestyles of Jews were becoming increasingly similar to their non-Jewish neighbors'. Jews were becoming solidly middle class in economic terms and were feeling secure enough to become actively involved in social and political causes.

There was no question that postwar America was good for the Jews. But was it good for Judaism?

By the 1950's the Judaism brought across the Atlantic by immigrants had become thoroughly Americanized. The suburban synagogue building boom, the growth of the Conservative and

This tallit collar, made by Rabbi Vicki Lieberman, includes a quotation from Hosea 2:19. The verse teaches that God promised to marry the Israelites in righteousness and justice. How might this teaching have inspired Jews to become activists?

Reform movements, and the increasing numbers of Jewish youth receiving some kind of Jewish education were hopeful signs for Judaism.

But beneath the surface, the warning signs were clear. The new synagogues were filled only on the High Holidays. Many afternoon religious schools seemed to create resentment among their students rather than enthusiasm for Jewish learning and life. Rituals that were still widely observed in the ethnic city neighborhoods before World War II, like observing Shabbat and keeping kosher, were increasingly being abandoned. Worst of all, American Judaism seemed to lack meaning and importance for some members of the younger generation.

Ironically, perhaps it was the success and acceptance of Jews and Judaism in America that created new challenges. With greater social acceptance, intermarriage rates were rising. As American Jews became more educated and wealthier, they were marrying later and having fewer children. These trends were summed up in a 1964 article in *Look* magazine titled "The Vanishing American Jew." How American Jews would respond to these challenges will be told in chapter 13.

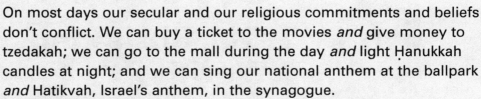
On most days our secular and our religious commitments and beliefs don't conflict. We can buy a ticket to the movies *and* give money to tzedakah; we can go to the mall during the day *and* light Ḥanukkah candles at night; and we can sing our national anthem at the ballpark *and* Hatikvah, Israel's anthem, in the synagogue.

But sometimes there *are* conflicts. Baseball superstars Hank Greenberg and Sandy Koufax each faced a conflict that required a major decision—to play or not to play on the Jewish High Holidays. In 1934, with his Detroit Tigers in a tight pennant race, Hank Greenberg decided to play on Rosh Hashanah, but not on Yom Kippur, by which time the Tigers had already clinched their division. In 1965 the Los Angeles Dodgers were in the World Series and wanted Sandy Koufax, their ace pitcher, to start Game 1. But the game fell on Yom Kippur—and Koufax decided not to pitch the game, which the Dodgers went on to lose.

The Dodgers slugger Shawn Green was yet another Jewish star to face this dilemma. In a key game in the 2004 play-off race, Green sat out the game on Yom Kippur.

1. Why was Greenberg's decision not to play on Yom Kippur an easier one to make than Koufax's and Green's decisions?

_____

_____

2. Do you think that Koufax and Green made the right decision? Why or why not?

_____

_____

_____

Chapter **11** The Diaspora Consolidates

Our Shrinking Jewish World

investigate

- What are the benefits of the Jewish population now being less spread out around the world?

- What are the disadvantages?

- What challenge does it create for the Jews of North America and Israel?

Key Words

Jews of Silence   Apartheid Laws

The **BIG** Picture

"The Jews are vanishing from Europe!"

This statement was not the jubilant claim of a fanatic antisemite, but rather the warning of the respected Jewish historian, Bernard Wasserstein, writing in 1996. Before World War II, he observed, Europe had been home to more than 9 million Jews. More than half of them died in the Holocaust.

European Jewry continued to decline—so much so that by 2005 there were only about 1.5 million Jews in Europe. Some died without having children to carry on the Jewish tradition; the rest moved elsewhere or abandoned their Jewish identities.

What happened in Europe was repeated in much of the rest of the Diaspora. Before World War II, Jews lived on six continents, in almost every country in the world. But since World War II, the Jewish world has rapidly shrunk. Today over 80 percent of world Jewry lives in just two countries: the United States and Israel. In fact, by 2005, half of all Jews lived in just five metropolitan areas: Tel Aviv, New York, Los Angeles, Haifa, and Jerusalem.

1948

Israeli ambassador Golda Meir visits Soviet Jews in Moscow

1959

Helen Suzman helps form anti-apartheid Progressive Party in South Africa

1967

World History:
First human heart transplant performed by Dr. Christiaan N. Barnard in South Africa

The Former Soviet Union

The Soviet Union emerged from World War II with the world's second-largest Jewish population—an estimated two million Jews. The only country with a larger Jewish population was the United States.

Joseph Stalin, leader of the Soviet Union, had begun to persecute Soviet Jews before World War II. After the war, he became even more extreme in his antisemitic policies. He ordered the murder of thousands of Jews, and was especially obsessed with executing Jewish intellectuals, writers, and artists.

1979

Islamic revolution over-throws government in Iran; thousands of Jews flee to escape persecution

1984

Operation Moses begins airlift of Ethiopian Jews to Israel

1991

Soviet Union col-lapses; hundreds of thousand of Soviet Jews leave for U.S. and Israel

1994

Terrorist bombing of Jewish Community Center in Buenos Aires, Argentina

Golda in Moscow

Just months after Israel declared its independence, Golda Myerson (Meir) traveled to Moscow as Israel's ambassador to the Soviet Union. It was October 1948, and she planned to attend Rosh Hashanah prayer services in the Great Synagogue in Moscow. But the Jews of the Soviet Union had been warned by the government to stay away. Stalin did not want them to publicly welcome Israel's ambassador or to openly celebrate Israeli independence.

As planned, she went to the synagogue on Rosh Hashanah. Meir later wrote, "Instead of the 2,000-odd Jews who usually came to the synagogue on the holidays, a crowd of close to 50,000 people was waiting for us…. They had come—those good, brave Jews—in order to be with us, to demonstrate their sense of kinship and to celebrate the establishment of the State of Israel." After an emotional service, Meir called out to the crowd in Yiddish: "Thank you for having remained Jews!"

Why do you think Soviet Jews were willing to risk being with Meir?

_____

_____

Why do you think Meir thanked them for remaining Jews?

_____

_____

Stalin's successor, Nikita Khrushchev, was openly critical of many of Stalin's violent policies—but not of his antisemitism. Although Khrushchev was less violent, he continued in Stalin's footsteps. He denied Jews the right to practice their faith, learn about their heritage, or move to another country. Khrushchev also severely limited Jews' access to top universities and government positions. In the words of Nobel Prize winner Elie Wiesel, the oppressed Russian Jews became the **Jews of Silence.**

Jews around the world responded. The State of Israel established a secret Liaison Bureau in 1952 to help Soviet Jews. Ḥabad-Lubavitch, a Ḥasidic movement, became involved in secret rescue efforts, as did new grassroots American Jewish organizations, such as the Student Struggle for Soviet Jewry, established in 1964. Civil rights activists joined the cause and Holocaust survivor Elie Wiesel traveled to Russia and wrote *The Jews of Silence* about his experiences.

This 1960's Pro-Soviet Jewry rally reflects the centuries-old tradition of Jews taking responsibility for the welfare of Jews who are in need.

But by 1967, following Israel's victory in the Six-Day War, growing numbers of Soviet Jews courageously challenged their government. They demanded religious and cultural rights, such as the right to participate in public prayer and to study Hebrew, as well as the right to move to another country. In response, they were fired from their jobs and, in some cases, also jailed.

In keeping with the religious teaching that all Jews are responsible for one another, Jews around the world—especially in North America and Israel—responded to the crisis by creating an international movement to free Soviet Jews. Their efforts included both public demonstrations and secret solidarity missions to the Soviet Union. They also lobbied governments to negotiate with Russia on behalf of the Jews.

Responding to this international pressure, the Soviet Union slowly opened its gates. Hundreds, then thousands, and then tens of thousands of Jews left before the fall of the Soviet Union in 1991—and many more have left in the years since. In total, more than one and a half million Jews left the former Soviet Union; by 2005, fewer than 400,000 Jews remained. Most of the emigrants settled in Israel or the United States.

Arab Lands

Before World War II, over one million Jews lived in Arab lands, such as Iraq, Syria, Egypt, North Africa, Yemen, and Morocco. Although Islamic law classified Jews as second-class citizens, many Eidot Hamizraḥ advanced economically and socially through the educational opportunities provided by Western countries and the Alliance Israélite Universelle, a French Jewish organization.

Arab nationalists often resented minority groups in the Arab world, Jews in particular. In North African countries like Algeria and Tunisia, this hatred was fueled by the Jews' eagerness to learn French and adopt French culture. Arab nationalists were struggling for their freedom from French rule and saw the Jews as French sympathizers. In response, they targeted local Jews as part of their campaign against Zionism.

Some Arab leaders, such as the Grand Mufti of Jerusalem, openly sided with Hitler during World War II. Anti-Jewish riots took place in major Arab cities in 1945 and again after the UN vote to partition Palestine in 1947. During the first two decades of Israel's existence, riots continued to take place, especially during the Arab-Israeli wars. In addition, in countries like Iraq, Jews were publicly hanged based on false charges of treason.

France's withdrawal from North Africa in the early 1960's threatened to make the situation

East Meets West, Jewish Style

The schools established by the Alliance Israélite Universelle in communities in North Africa, Morocco, and Iran introduced thousands of Jews to modern ideas and ways of life. They insisted that all students learn French and the local language, but they did not teach Judeo-Arabic, the Jewish language that many spoke at home. They also encouraged the Mizrahi Jews to wear Western clothing. Finally, they showed contempt for local Jewish rabbis and for religious practices that they considered superstitious or primitive. While the schools often distanced their students from traditional Judaism as practiced in Muslim lands, they did prepare them to work and prosper in the modern world.

Judaism survives not only because of the actions of adults but also because of the commitment of schoolchildren. In 1960, Miriam (right), a Tunisian Jew, wrote to the Joint Distribution Committee saying that she and several other girls wanted to learn Hebrew. The JDC responded by supplying them with books and other educational materials.

for Jews there even worse. The result was a dramatic exodus of Jews from the Arab Middle East, with most finding refuge in Israel and others in France, Canada, and the United States. By 2007 fewer than eight thousand Jews lived in Arab countries, once home to more than one million Jews.

Iran

Jews have lived in Persia (where modern Iran is located) for twenty-six hundred years, since our ancestors were first exiled to Babylonia. The biblical story of Purim, told in the Book of Esther, took place there, and the country remained home to thousands of Jews into modern times. Its Jewish population in 1945 was estimated at ninety thousand. Under the favorable rule of Mohammad Reza Shah Pahlavi (1941–1979), who believed in modernization and ties with the West, the Iranian Jews flourished.

The Iranian Jewish community is said to have been one of the wealthiest and most highly educated Jewish communities in the world. The capital, Tehran, boasted Jewish schools, active social and cultural organizations, and some thirty synagogues. Iran and Israel maintained close relations.

All of this changed following the Islamic revolution in Iran in 1979. As Iran turned away from the West and its modern influences, and came under Islamic religious control, persecution of Jews increased, as did anti-Israel sympathies. Security, freedom, and progress for Jews gave way to insecurity, anxiety, and loss of status.

The leading figure in Iran's Jewish community, Habib Elqānyān, was charged with pro-Zionist activities and was executed in 1979. In 1999 thirteen Jews in Shiraz were arrested on charges of spying for Israel. By then, many Jews had left the country, and by 2005 the Jewish population of Iran was estimated at only eleven thousand. Today, there are large communities of Iranian Jews in the United States, those in Southern California among them.

Zelig Bub, a Latvian Jew, settled in South Africa in 1927. His great-grandchildren have kept his Latvian passport as a keepsake of their family history. Describe a family keepsake, such as a photograph or decorative object, that you or other relatives have.

South Africa

South African Jewry numbered about 100,000 after World War II. Most came from Lithuania and moved to South Africa in search of a better life. In a country that divided its people by race and treated them unequally, Jews enjoyed the privilege that came with being white. Blacks, by contrast, lived in poverty, suffering under South Africa's infamous **apartheid laws** designed to keep people of different races from mixing.

Some Jews courageously joined the battle to fight apartheid and suffered for it. Others believed that radical political change would be harmful to Jews and supported the government. Still others urged gradual moderate change, fearing social revolution.

Apartheid officially ended in 1994 and Nelson Mandela became South Africa's first black president. Under Mandela, many laws designed to benefit the country's oppressed and underprivileged blacks were introduced. For Jews, though, the new

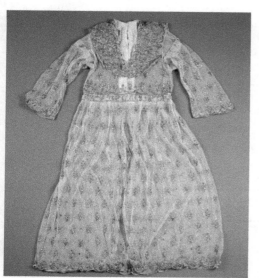

Wedding dress of Jewish bride, Persia, late nineteenth or early twentieth century. As the size and number of Diaspora communities become smaller, some of the richness and diversity of Jewish life and tradition are at risk of being lost.

Helen Suzman

Helen Suzman

Helen Suzman was born on November 7, 1917, in the mining town of Germiston, South Africa. Her parents, Lithuanian Jewish immigrants, had come to South Africa to escape the oppression of Jews in Russia. In 1948, when the pro-apartheid National Party came to power, Suzman joined the moderate United Party and was elected to Parliament in 1953. Six years later, along with eleven other liberal members of Parliament, Suzman helped form the anti-apartheid Progressive Party. Of the twelve founding members, only she was reelected to Parliament in 1961.

For the next thirteen years, Suzman was the sole anti-apartheid member of Parliament. Once criticized by another member of Parliament for embarrassing South Africa abroad because of the questions she raised about the government's discriminatory policies, Suzman responded, "It is not *my questions* that embarrass South Africa—it is *your answers.*"

As white opposition to apartheid grew, Suzman eventually was joined in Parliament by white, liberal colleagues. She retired from Parliament in 1989 but was at Nelson Mandela's side in 1996 when he signed South Africa's new constitution.

Describe one Jewish value that Helen Suzman honored in her fight against apartheid.

_____

Why might it be important to non-Jews for Jews to become educated about and committed to Jewish values and traditions?

_____

_____

South Africa proved to be a more difficult place to live and work.

A great many jobs were now reserved for black people and, as often happens when a country goes through social and political upheaval, crime rates soared. In addition, the new government was highly critical of Israel. As a result, many Jews left South Africa, particularly younger Jews. From a peak of around 117,000 Jews, the Jewish population declined to 75,000 in the early years of the twenty-first century.

Latin America

Jews were legally barred from settling in most Central and South American countries until well into the nineteenth century. Some Jews, known as crypto-Jews, had come to the region three hundred years earlier, from Spain and Portugal, and practiced Judaism secretly. Many of them, especially in Peru and Mexico, later became victims of the Inquisition, a court set up by the Catholic Church to investigate people who disagreed with Church teachings and rulings. Dutch, British, and Danish Caribbean colonies, being non-Catholic, permitted Jews to establish synagogues and communities openly. The majority of Latin America's Jews, however, arrived in more modern times.

Four waves of Jews arrived in Latin America: East European Jews during the era of mass immigration; Sephardic Jews from the Ottoman Empire as it disintegrated; Jews who could not get into the United States after most immigration was cut off in 1924; and German Jews escaping Hitler. To some extent these groups remained separate from one another,

This poster for the American-Yiddish film *Tevye der Miliger* (Tevye the Dairyman) was created for Latin American audiences around 1940.

particularly Yiddish-speaking Ashkenazic Jews and Ladino-speaking Sephardic Jews.

Today, Argentina has the largest Latin American Jewish community. Most Jews in Argentina and throughout Latin America live in large cities. They form distinctive communities, often with their own schools and institutions, keeping much more separate from their non-Jewish neighbors than Jews in the United States, although increasing numbers participate in the general Latin American culture.

Antisemitism has long been characteristic of Latin American life. After World War II, Argentina became a haven for Nazis, and throughout Latin America Jews have been accused by those on the political right of being Communists and radicals, even as they are condemned by Communists for being capitalists.

More than 100,000 Jews have left Argentina in recent years. This exodus has been due partly to the 1992 terrorist bombings of the Israeli embassy in Buenos Aires and the 1994 bombings of the Jewish Community Center, and is also a result of Argentina's economic problems.

Other significant Jewish communities in Latin America can be found in Brazil, Mexico, Chile, Uruguay, and Venezuela.

The New Face of World Jewry

By 2005, about 97.4 percent of all Jews lived in just fifteen countries.

Millions of Jews have migrated since the end of World War II. For the most part, they have abandoned underdeveloped, unstable, and dangerous countries such as the Soviet Union, Ethiopia, and South Africa, moving to wealthy and politically stable countries that are more tolerant of Jews. About 90 percent of world Jewry now lives in these more economically and socially attractive countries. As a result, no major Jewish community suffers widespread persecution. In addition, because so many Jews live close to one another, they benefit from strength of numbers. Jewish citizens of larger communities can work together to realize common goals.

The negative impact of this shift in population is that most of the world outside of these major Jewish communities no longer has first-hand knowledge of Jews and Judaism. Instead of its former role as a world religion, Judaism is now a regional religion. Where once Jews were found all over the world, since World War II they have increasingly tended to settle in a limited number of places, centered in the world's wealthiest and most advanced countries.

Centers of World Jewish Population
Reported in the *American Jewish Year Book,* 2005

◎ United States	5,280,000	◎ Australia	102,000
◎ Israel	5,237,600	◎ Brazil	96,700
◎ France	494,000	◎ Ukraine	84,000
◎ Canada	372,000	◎ South Africa	72,500
◎ United Kingdom	297,000	◎ Hungary	49,900
◎ Russia	235,000	◎ Mexico	39,800
◎ Argentina	185,000	◎ Belgium	31,200
◎ Germany	115,000		

For centuries, Jews lived in Ethiopia but were cut off from the rest of our people. In Ethiopia these Jews were ill-treated and lived in poverty; many were malnourished. Most worked in farming, but they were also well known for their fine crafts and jewelry.

When Ethiopia suffered a great famine and war in the 1980's, the Jews became especially eager to leave. In 1984, the Israeli government and Jewish organizations from North America worked with the Israeli Airline, El Al, to fly these Jews from Ethiopia to Israel. Because the Ethiopian government did not want the world to know that almost eight thousand of its citizens were fleeing the country, the rescue mission had to be secret.

The mission to bring the Ethiopian Jews to Israel continued into the 1990's. Almost the entire Jewish community of Ethiopia has been brought to Israel. Today more than fifty-six thousand Ethiopians live in the Jewish state.

1. Describe one benefit of the relocation of Jews from Ethiopia to Israel.

_____

_____

_____

2. Describe one disadvantage of the relocation.

_____

_____

_____

Chapter 12 Israel in Our Time

An Ongoing Story of Challenge and Triumph

investigate

- What are some of the achievements of the modern State of Israel?

- What are the sources of Israel's ongoing conflict with Palestinians?

- What compromises has Israel been willing to make to reach a lasting peace?

- How might peace in Israel enrich the lives of Diaspora Jews?

Key Words

Sabras	Six-Day War
Operation Moses	Gush Emunim
Operation Solomon	Intifada
Beta Israel	Palestine Liberation Organization
Law of Return	Second Intifada
Knesset	Hamas
Israel Defense Forces (IDF)	Hezbollah

The BIG Picture

The modern State of Israel is a place of contrasts, none greater than the contrast between old and new. Emek Refaim, where King David drove out the Philistines, is now a bustling Jerusalem avenue, filled with cafés, hamburger joints, and trendy clothing stores. Similarly, at the foot of Mount Tabor, where Barak and the prophet Deborah gathered the Israelite army, lies the modern village of Kfar Tavor.

Travel on a city bus and other contrasts come to light. A Ḥasidic Jew in his distinctive black hat sits next to a bareheaded teen. An Armenian priest gestures to an Arab woman in a long embroidered dress to open the window. And a young Israeli soldier from Ethiopia offers an elderly tourist her seat.

Israel's mixture of old and new and its religious and cultural diversity are just a few of its truly amazing wonders. But Israel also continually has faced one challenge that has dominated all others: the need to make peace with its Arab neighbors and with the Palestinians.

1967	1973	1979	1987	1989
Six-Day War	Yom Kippur War	Israel and Egypt sign peace treaty	Palestinian Intifada begins in Gaza and West Bank	**World History:** World Wide Web invented

New Immigrants

Israel is a country of seven million, made up of 77 percent Jews, 19 percent Arabs, and 4 percent others. Two-thirds of its Jewish population are native-born Israelis, or *sabras.* Earlier chapters discussed how hundreds of thousands of European and Mizraḥi refugees immigrated to Israel in the late 1940's and 1950's. More recent waves of immigrants have arrived from Ethiopia and the former Soviet Union. They are changing the face of Israel just as Israel has changed them.

Large numbers of Ethiopian Jews began to arrive in the 1970's. Many of the eighty-five thousand Ethiopians living in Israel by the early twenty-first century were rescued from their war-torn, famine-stricken country in two airlifts known as **Operation Moses** in 1984 and **Operation Solomon** in 1991. Thousands of Ethiopian Jews who converted to Christianity in the past but have since returned to Judaism are still waiting to be brought to Israel.

1994

Israel and Jordan sign peace treaty

2000

Second Intifada begins

2005

Jewish settlements removed from Gaza Strip

2006

Hamas wins Palestinian elections

Beta Israel

Ethiopian Jews call their community Beta Israel (the House of Israel), although other Ethiopians refer to them as Falashas ("strangers" or "foreigners"). According to their own traditions, they trace their lineage back to King Solomon and the Queen of Sheba. But genetic tests indicate that they are descended from native Ethiopians who converted to Judaism or intermarried with Jewish traders from Yemen.

At first, the Ethiopians were greeted with an outpouring of warmth, but their integration into Israeli life often has not been smooth. Some have complained of Israelis' prejudice. But the biggest barrier has been the Ethiopians' lack of education and job skills, which has made it difficult for them to find work.

The largest number of recent immigrants to Israel has come from the former Soviet Union. Between 1989 and 2000 almost 900,000 arrived. Some left the former Soviet Union fearing the rising antisemitism, but many more came in search of greater economic opportunity.

These immigrants generally have been highly educated and skilled. Russian doctors have brought their expertise to Israeli hospitals,

A Jewish prayer service in Ethiopia

Russian athletes and coaches have strengthened Israel's professional sports and Olympics teams, and Russian engineers have contributed to Israel's electronics and high-tech boom.

Yet Russian immigration has brought its own challenges. Many well-educated Russians have not found employment in the kinds of skilled professions and jobs they once had. But the greatest problems have arisen over religious issues and Jewish identity.

Israel's **Law of Return** grants automatic citizenship to the families of all immigrants with a Jewish grandparent. But these new citizens often find that they are not considered Jewish in regard to more personal matters—such as marriage and burial rites. These matters are governed by the stricter Jewish law that requires one's mother to be Jewish. By that standard, about one-third of Russian immigrants are non-Jews. In such cases, unless they convert to Judaism with an Orthodox rabbi, Israeli rabbis are prohibited from performing their marriages and they are not permitted to be buried in Jewish cemeteries.

A Religious or Secular Country?

About 20 percent of Israel's Jewish population consider themselves religious, and another 35 percent describe themselves as "traditionalists" but do not strictly observe Jewish law. The remaining 45 percent consider themselves non-religious, or secular. Religious and secular Jews work side by side and share the same public spaces. Usually they get along, but they often disagree on how Israel should balance its Western-style democracy with its Jewish character.

Should all aspects of Israeli life be determined by Jewish religious law? Should Israel become a completely secular country where Jewish law and tradition have no special influence? Or, should Israel find a balance between these two views?

Since the founding of the modern State of Israel, the government has accepted certain basic policies regarding Judaism's role in Israeli society. Saturday is observed as the official day of rest. Jewish holidays, like Passover and Rosh Hashanah, are recognized as official state holidays. And kosher food is served in all army kitchens and in government buildings. In addition, there are religious political parties, which use their influence in the **Knesset**—Israel's legislature—to strengthen Israel's observance of Jewish law.

Especially problematic to secular Israelis is the religious court's control over personal status issues—marriage, divorce, funerals, and religious conversion. It requires that all Jewish marriages and conversions conducted in Israel be performed by Orthodox rabbis. Secular resentment is further inflamed by the many ultra-Orthodox young men who use student exemptions to avoid serving in the **Israel Defense Forces (IDF).**

What Do You Think?

Buses are the most popular form of public transportation in Israel. Yet most bus service comes to a halt on Shabbat and major Jewish holidays. Orthodox Jews generally support this policy, arguing that it enriches Israel's Jewish character. But many secular Jews see it as imposing on their personal freedom, saying that most Israelis are secular and that the rule discriminates against poor people who cannot afford automobiles.

With which position do you agree? Why?

_____

_____

_____

Whatever differences of opinion there are, most Jewish Israelis agree that the state should be influenced by Jewish traditions and values. In contrast, Israel's Arab community sees the Jewish nature of the state as a barrier to their acceptance as full and equal citizens.

A Shifting Economy

The communal way of life and "back to the soil" ideology of *kibbutzim* made them the pride of Israel's Socialist pioneers. Parents and children lived separately, members ate in communal dining halls, and members' earnings were based on their needs.

But this lifestyle no longer appealed to the younger generation of the 1980's. This resulted in *kibbutzim* moving children back in with their parents. Many also stopped serving meals in dining halls. And some began to base salaries on the status of different jobs, so that a factory worker no longer earned as much as a manager.

Israel's national economic policies are changing, too. There is more private-company competition, and some companies that had been owned by the government have been sold to private investors. In addition, the arrival of highly skilled workers from the former Soviet Union combined with the possibility of peace with Israel's Arab neighbors helped create a technology boom in the mid-1990's. Israeli companies have become leaders in the areas of software, communications, and biotechnology.

Economic growth has brought prosperity to many. But it also has widened the gap between rich and poor. While Israelis have more choices regarding what and where to spend their money, the neediest receive less government

Many Israelis are attracted to Western pop culture, including Western dress, music, fast food, and technology. Often it seems as if their eyes are set on the American dream rather than on the Zionist dream. How might Israel benefit from becoming Americanized? How might such Americanization take away from Israel's special character?

help than in the 1950's and 1960's. By the early twenty-first century, 20 percent of Israelis were living below the poverty line.

The Six-Day War

Israel has experienced more than its share of bloodshed and war. In May 1967, Egyptian president Gamal Abdel-Nasser blockaded the Straits of Tiran, stopping all ships from entering or leaving Israel's southern port of Eilat. He massed troops along the border with Israel. Expecting war, Israel struck first, launching a daring air attack against Egypt.

Israel's first strike on the morning of June 5 destroyed the Egyptian air force. Syria and Jordan entered the war on Egypt's side but were quickly defeated. In what became known as the **Six-Day War,** Israel captured the Sinai Desert and Gaza Strip from Egypt, the West Bank from Jordan, and the Golan Heights from Syria. In addition, it gained control of East Jerusalem, including the Old City. Jerusalem was united.

The Hebrew word for cell phones is *pelefonim,* literally meaning "wonder phones." Looking at this photograph, can you figure out how to say "telephones" and "Internet" in Hebrew?

Jerusalem

Liberating the Western Wall

Imagine that you are an Israeli paratrooper in the Six-Day War. After fierce fighting, you receive the signal to take the Old City of Jerusalem. On June 7 you and your comrades enter, meeting little Arab resistance at the Lion's Gate. You race to the Temple Mount and the Western Wall, a supporting wall of the ancient Temple. The army's chief chaplain, General Rabbi Shlomo Goren, blows a long *t'ki'ah* on a shofar to announce the Jews' return to their holiest site after almost two thousand years. You raise the Israeli flag from atop the Western Wall.

Why do you think this was such an emotional moment, not only for those who were present but also for Jews in the Diaspora?

_____

_____

_____

The most emotional moment in the war was the liberation of the Western Wall, or *Kotel,* and the reunification of East and West Jerusalem.

The Problems Continue

The new territories tripled Israel's size. They also prevented Egyptian and Syrian rockets from being placed where they could reach Israel's major cities. But controlling the territories created two new problems: first, the Jewish settlements that were established in formerly Arab lands, and second, the one million Palestinian Arabs who lived in the newly occupied territories. These problems plague Israel to this day.

Religious Zionists like Rabbi Zvi Yehudah Kook believed that Israel's victory was a sign that the coming of the Messiah was near. His students helped found **Gush Emunim** (Bloc of the Faithful), which opposed returning any of the captured land and declared that Jews had a right to the entire biblical land of Israel. Other Israelis warned that ruling a people against their will would violate Jewish values and weaken Israel.

The UN and most countries, including the United States, believed that the return of territories would be part of any future peace agreements between Israel and the Arabs, and that Jewish settlements would make Israel's withdrawal more difficult.

At first, the Israeli government limited Jewish settlement to areas that were critical to national security or had great religious significance. But by the late 1970's, an Israeli government was elected that encouraged settlements in areas that had previously been off-limits. By 2006, about 200,000 Jews—both secular and religious—were living in the West Bank and Golan Heights.

At the same time, high birthrates increased the Palestinian Arab population in the territories from one million in 1967 to almost three million by the early twenty-first century. Frustrated and angered by Israeli occupation and settlement, Palestinian Arabs sought independence. The West Bank and Gaza became a time bomb.

In December 1987 a Palestinian uprising began in Gaza and the West Bank. It became known as the **Intifada,** or "shaking off." Starting with demonstrations, it escalated into rock-throwing and, eventually, into the use of homemade explosives. To much of the world, Palestinians had become the heroic "David" standing up to the "Goliath," Israel.

Palestine Liberation Organization

Palestinian resistance groups outside of the West Bank were committed to Israel's destruction. The Palestine Liberation Organization (PLO) was founded in 1964. Yasir Arafat, who became chairman in 1969, used acts of terror, targeting innocent civilians to gain sympathy for the Palestinian cause. Although most Palestinians were not terrorists, many began to support the PLO in their belief that Arafat would liberate them.

New Hope

In October 1973, Egypt and Syria surprised Israel with an attack on Yom Kippur.

Israeli casualties were high, but the IDF eventually triumphed. Then a breakthrough in Israel's relations with its neighbors came in November 1977 when Egyptian president Anwar Sadat flew to Jerusalem to address the Knesset, Israel's parliament: "I declare to the whole world that we accept to live with you in a permanent peace based on justice."

Israel's Prime Minister Menaḥem Begin agreed to withdraw from Sinai and in 1979 the leaders signed a peace treaty. Although two years later Sadat was assassinated by Islamic extremists opposed to his peace efforts, the treaty has held. In 1994, Israel and Jordan, which had long maintained secret relations, also signed a formal treaty.

A breakthrough in Israel's conflict with the Palestinians almost came in 1993. The PLO and its chairman Yasir Arafat renounced terrorism and recognized Israel's right to exist. In return, Israel's prime minister Yitzḥak Rabin recognized the PLO as the representative of the Palestinian people. On September 13, 1993, both sides signed an agreement to end fighting and extend self-rule to the Palestinians in parts of Gaza and the West Bank.

Peace Remains a Dream

Despite the agreement and high hopes, the conflict continued and tensions rose in Israel. Rabin was denounced as a traitor at anti-government rallies even though a majority of Israelis supported his policies. On November 4, 1995, shortly after attending a peace rally, Rabin was assassinated by a Jewish extremist, Yigal Amir, who opposed the peace process.

U.S. president Bill Clinton brought both sides together in the summer of 2000 in the hope of stopping the violence and shaping a final agreement. But the negotiations broke down and the West Bank and Gaza soon broke out in the **Second Intifada,** more violent and deadly than the first. Suicide bombers brought the violence into the heart of Israel, targeting cafés, nightclubs, and hotels.

To protect its citizens, in 2002 Israel began building a security fence separating much of the West Bank from Israel. Two years later, the violence was quieting down and Arafat died,

Palestinian boys throwing stones at an Israeli tank in the West Bank city of Jenin

Yitzḥak Rabin

Yitzḥak Rabin (1922–1995) was a senior military commander before becoming prime minister. During his first term (1974–1977) he ordered a daring raid on the air-port in Entebbe, Uganda, after terrorists hijacked an Air France jetliner there. The raid freed all but 3 of the 105 Jews who were held hostage. In Rabin's second term

Standing with their Nobel Peace Prize, from left to right: Yasir Arafat, Shimon Peres, and Yitzḥak Rabin

(1992–1995), he shifted his goals from winning wars to winning peace. In 1994, Rabin, Shimon Peres (a former Israeli prime minister), and Yasir Arafat jointly were awarded the Nobel Prize for Peace for their efforts to bring peace to the Middle East.

After negotiating the peace agreement with Arafat in 1993, Rabin said, "I would have liked to sign a peace agreement with Holland, or Luxembourg, or New Zealand. But there was no need to…. One does not make peace with one's friends. One makes peace with one's enemies."

What do you think Rabin meant?

_____

_____

_____

How can you apply this idea to your life?

_____

_____

_____

removing what many Israelis considered to be an obstacle to peace. Israeli prime minister Ariel Sharon, once a leading supporter of settlements, became convinced that Israel could not hold on to the Gaza Strip and most of the West Bank. In 2005 he evacuated the Jewish settlements in Gaza and pulled out the army.

But efforts to advance the peace process were hurt by the victory of **Hamas** (an Islamic resistance movement) in the 2006 Palestinian elections. Hamas gained the support of many Palestinians through its promise to end the corruption that had existed under the PLO and by providing medical care, schools, and other social services. But it also carried out many terror attacks in Israel and was committed to Israel's destruction.

Efforts to negotiate a peace between Israel and Syria have thus far also failed, and Israel's northern border with Lebanon has been a constant source of problems. Lebanon is a weak country unable to prevent militant groups from using its southern region to launch attacks on Israel. In June 1982, Israel invaded Lebanon to drive out the PLO, which had taken hold of southern Lebanon. Israel's campaign was successful, but at a high cost in both Lebanese civilian and Israeli lives.

The war and Israel's continued occupation of a security zone in southern Lebanon until May 2000 were among the key factors that led to the creation of **Hezbollah** (Party of God), an Islamist political party and militant group. Hezbollah played on the resentment that some Lebanese felt toward Israel, and, like Hamas in Gaza, it won support by meeting critical social needs, such as running hospitals and schools.

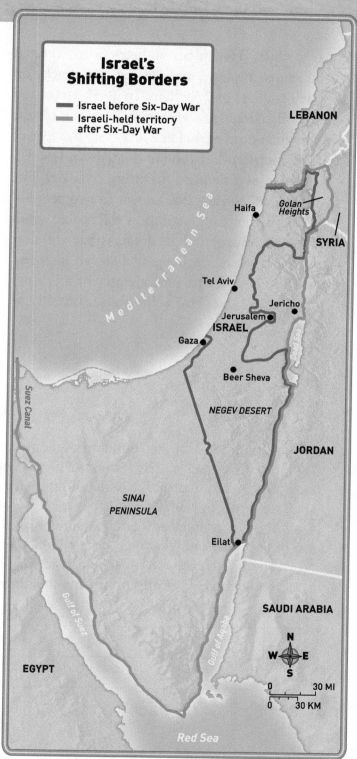

As a result of the Six-Day War in 1967, the area under Israeli control was expanded to include Gaza, the West Bank, and the Sinai Peninsula.

Meanwhile, Hezbollah fighters were trained and armed by Iran, and carried out attacks on Israeli soldiers and civilians. In 2006, Israel and Hezbollah fought a war with no clear results other than considerable destruction and loss of life in southern Lebanon and northern Israel.

Are hopes for a peaceful future realistic? The Arab-Israeli conflict boils down to two peoples' claims on one land. A solution will require both sides to compromise on dreams that are dear and beliefs that are deep. Whatever happens, you will not read the next chapter of this story in a history book. You will watch it unfold day by day.

Despite years of friction between Arabs and Jews, there are signs that someday peace may become more than a dream. Here Abu Sway (center), a Palestinian, and Israeli children play soccer together at the Japanese-Israeli-Palestinian Friendship Soccer Match.

Revisiting Herzl's Hope

Herzl imagined that the founding of a Jewish State would solve the problem of anti-semitism. But today, *The Protocols of the Elders of Zion* is sold on the streets of Cairo and Damascus. Extremist leaders in Iran say that the Holocaust is a "myth," and they call for Israel to be "wiped off the map." Although many Jewish Israelis agree that they might be safer in Miami or Los Angeles, in the same breath they would sing the lyrics to the popular Israeli song, "I Have No Other Country."

Why do you think both secular and religious Jews continue to remain in Israel despite the many challenges and hardships they face?

_____

_____

_____

The prophet Isaiah had a beautiful vision of a time when there would be no more wars. He wrote, "And they shall beat their swords into plowshares, and their spears into pruning hooks; nation shall not lift up sword against nation, neither shall they learn war any more" (Isaiah 2:4).

Yitzḥak Rabin heeded these words when he extended his hand to Yasir Arafat and declared, "Let us pray that a day will come when we all will say: 'Farewell to arms.'"

Send a postcard or an e-mail to the prime minister of Israel or an Arab leader. Describe in words or draw a picture of what you think Israel will look like when there is peace between the Jews and their neighbors.

AIR MAIL

Chapter 13 American Jewry Today

Making the Choice to Survive and Thrive

investigate

- What are some of the ways in which American Jews are diverse?
- What are some of the challenges facing American Jews?
- What might some solutions be?

Key Words

Holocaust Remembrance Day

American Israel Public Affairs Committee (AIPAC)

Egalitarian

Havurah Movement

Jewish Renewal Movement

The BIG Picture

On June 3, 1972, Sally Priesand became the first woman to be publicly ordained, or graduated from a religious seminary, as a rabbi. She and other women who followed in her path became role models for thousands of girls and symbols of the Jewish feminist movement.

At about the same time, another woman was setting out on a lifelong quest to change the Jewish world for the better. Esther Jungreis was a generation older than Priesand, a Holocaust survivor, and an Orthodox Jew. In 1972 she issued a call for "a rally of souls at Madison Square Garden, a mass spiritual gathering where you teach people what it means to be a Jew." She electrified thousands with her stories, and led the gathering in a mass recitation of the Sh'ma. Jungreis continued to spread her message through books, the Internet, and television programs.

What do Priesand and Jungreis have in common? A lot, actually. They each symbolize the energy and diversity within today's North American Jewish community.

1960	1969	Early 1970's	1972
English-language edition of *Night* by Elie Wiesel published	"Freedom Seder" held in Washington, D.C.	Havurah movement gains strength	Sally Priesand becomes first woman publicly ordained as a rabbi

Jewish Pride

During the late 1960's and early 1970's, Americans began to take a growing interest in exploring their ethnic and racial heritage. There was an increasing acceptance and celebration of the ethnic differences in American society. American Jews expressed their pride by openly wearing *magen David* pendants, often called "Jewish stars," and *kippot*.

The publication of the English-language edition of Elie Wiesel's book *Night*, in 1960, helped make Holocaust remembrance a top priority among American Jews. When in May of that same year, Israeli agents in Buenos Aires, Argentina, arrested Adolf Eichmann, notorious manager of the plan to systematically kill all European Jewry, Holocaust awareness rose even higher. Eichmann was brought to trial in Israel. As American Jews followed the trial, they began to openly discuss their memories of the Holocaust.

In the following decades, **Holocaust Remembrance Day,** *Yom Hashoah*, gained widespread observance. The Holocaust became the subject of study in secular and religious school classrooms throughout North America.

1991	1993	2001	2006
Shoshanah Cardin becomes first female chair of Conference of Presidents of Major Jewish Organizations	U.S. Holocaust Memorial Museum opens in Washington, D.C.	Terrorist attacks on September 11 kill 3,000 people	**World History:** International Astronomical Union demotes Pluto to the status of a "dwarf planet"

By the late 1980's, there were twelve Holocaust memorials and nineteen museums dedicated to Holocaust remembrance in the United States. The U.S. Holocaust Memorial Museum, a project of the federal government, opened in Washington, D.C., in 1993. That same year, Steven Spielberg's film about the Holocaust, *Schindler's List*, won top honors at the Academy Awards.

American Jews' Connection with Israel

Just seven years after the arrest of Eichmann, American Jewry was again confronted with the possible destruction of millions of Jews. In the weeks leading up to the June 1967 Six-Day War, they listened to Egyptian president Gamal Abdel Nasser's anti-Israel propaganda and his threats to destroy the young Jewish State. Israel's extraordinary victory caused American Jews to swell with ethnic pride.

Israel Independence Day Parade participants expressing their support of Israel. How can you show your support?

American Jews' deep concern for Israel's survival was reflected in the hundreds of millions of dollars they contributed on its behalf. But tzedakah was not the only way American Jews expressed their identification with the Jewish state. In the years after 1967, American Jewish tourism to Israel increased. Zionism and Israeli history were taught almost universally in Jewish schools. And the organized American Jewish community began a tireless campaign in support of Israel. Reflecting the increasing importance of Israel to American Jews, the **American Israel Public Affairs Committee (AIPAC)** grew into a powerful lobbying organization, dedicated to influencing U.S. foreign policy in support of Israel.

But, in recent years, there has been increasing concern about the relationship between American and Israeli Jews. One issue is the wedge between some American and Israeli Jews that is due to differing views on how to address the Israeli-Arab conflict. Other sources of friction include the Israeli government's refusal to give legal status to non-Orthodox movements—for example, its refusal to permit non-Orthodox rabbis to perform Jewish wedding ceremonies or conversions.

Recent polls have registered a decline in American Jewish identification with Israel, especially among the young. American Jewish leaders hope that ties between the two communities can be strengthened through the visits of American Jews to Israel as tourists and as participants in volunteer projects and study programs.

Jewish Activism

Since the late 1960's, when some Jewish civil rights activists began to explore how Judaism could help them live more meaningful lives, the teachings of prophetic Judaism and *tikun olam*—acts of social justice—have grown in popularity among American Jews. Jewish sacred texts have inspired many to pursue justice and help the poor in a variety of ways, including voter registration and literacy

Today, many liberal synagogues sponsor social action projects and their religious schools require students to participate in *tikun olam* projects.

Social Justice and Passover

Members of Jews for Urban Justice, a group that fought against poverty and other forms of social injustice, found a modern way to express the strong ties between social justice and Judaism. The third day of Passover in 1969 was the first anniversary of the assassination of civil rights leader Dr. Martin Luther King, Jr. Jews for Urban Justice held a "freedom seder" in the basement of an African American church. A diverse crowd of Jews and non-Jews sat at tables set with a traditional seder plate. They read from a haggadah that combined traditional prayers with readings on the themes of freedom and struggle for social justice in America.

Describe one way in which the story of the Israelites' escape from slavery is similar to a struggle that Jews or another people are experiencing today.

_____

_____

At your family's seder table, how can you connect current events to the story of the Exodus?

_____

_____

Shoshana S. Cardin

Shoshanah Cardin visiting a Jewish community in the mountains of Azerbaijan

Shoshana Cardin was born in Tel Aviv in 1926. Her family moved to Baltimore, Maryland, when she was three. Her life has been guided by the value of community service. As a child, Cardin gave political speeches, raised money for the Jewish National Fund, and was elected president of her Zionist youth group. As an adult, she became a feminist, civic leader, and social activist.

Cardin was the first female president of the Council of Jewish Federations in 1984; the first female chair of the National Council of Soviet Jewry in 1988; and the first female chair of the Conference of Presidents of Major American Jewish Organizations in 1991. In 2003, she became the chair of the Shoshana S. Cardin Jewish Community High School in Baltimore. She has also been the chairwoman of secular organizations, such as the Maryland Commission for Women and the Maryland Volunteer Network.

Cardin's many accomplishments include helping to provide services for women with financial credit needs and for battered women. Through her negotiations with world leaders, such as George Bush and Soviet president Mikhail Gorbachev, she has helped to gain aid to Israel and to Soviet Jews who want to move to Israel.

Some leaders become famous throughout the world. Others are known only within their own community. Name a modern Jewish woman whom you admire for her leadership or her social, political, or religious activism. Explain why you admire her.

_____

_____

programs, Peace Corps agricultural projects, and synagogue High Holiday food drives.

Jewish Feminism

By the early 1970's, the Jewish community began to recognize ways in which Judaism treated women and men differently. The Jewish feminist movement was born, seeking to make Judaism **egalitarian** by adapting it so that women and men were treated with equality.

This was a time when women were achieving greater equality in the American workplace and within the larger culture. Thus, it seemed increasingly inappropriate and out-of-date that men and women were treated differently in synagogue. At that time, women were not permitted to be ordained as rabbis. In most synagogues, women were not permitted to receive an *aliyah* (the honor of reciting the Torah reading blessings) or to be counted in a minyan, the quorum of ten Jewish adults required for a prayer service.

By the late twentieth century, with the exception of the Orthodox movement, Jewish women were permitted to participate equally in most aspects of synagogue life. They could be called to the Torah for an *aliyah*, counted in the minyan, and serve as synagogue board members and congregation presidents.

By the 1970's and 1980's, some Orthodox women began to organize women's prayer groups in their synagogues, where they read from the

Sally J. Priesand, the first woman to be ordained by the Reform movement. Sandy Sasso was ordained by the Reconstructionist movement in 1977, and in 1985 the Conservative movement ordained Amy Eilberg.

Gay and Lesbian Equality

In the 1980's, a new front opened in the continuing tug-of-war between tradition and modernity, this time over establishing the equality of lesbians and gay men. Synagogues whose members were largely lesbian and gay were founded in major urban centers during the 1970's and 1980's. But as gays and lesbians pushed for greater acceptance in American society, they also wanted to be included in mainstream Jewish life. By 1984 the Reconstructionist Rabbinical College voted to admit openly gay and lesbian students and by the 1990's mainstream synagogues were becoming more welcoming to lesbians and gays. In the past few years, some liberal rabbis have begun to officiate at same-sex commitment ceremonies and marriages, and the Reform movement has established a center for the study of sexuality and gender.

But the issue of gay and lesbian equality within Judaism continues to be debated. Opponents argue that Jewish law allows for no compromise on this issue.

Torah. A few began to put on prayer shawls, or *tallitot*. And today, many more Orthodox women have advanced education in Jewish studies. While most Orthodox rabbis continue to believe that Jewish law prevents women from being ordained, the role and religious authority of women in the modern Orthodox community continues to expand.

Orthodox Judaism

In the mid-twentieth century, the American Orthodox community seemed to be shrinking in size. But as American society became more tolerant of diversity, Orthodox Jews have found greater acceptance. The result has been increased observance of rituals, such as keeping kosher and attending synagogue, and significant growth in Orthodox day school education. In addition, most children who grow up Orthodox are choosing to remain within the movement as adults. The movement's increased strength is also due to Orthodox couples tending to have large families.

The Ḥasidic community and the ultra-Orthodox yeshiva world are also flourishing. Both groups benefited from a wave of refugees from Europe immediately before and after World War II. Most choose to isolate themselves from the secular world by living in separate communities and creating their own business, social, and religious organizations.

Liberal Judaism

The Reform movement has grown in recent years. About 35 percent of American Jews identify themselves as Reform, making it the largest Jewish movement in the United States today. Two trends within the movement help account for this growth: increasing observance of Jewish tradition in ways that help families personalize and deepen their Jewish identities, and outreach to those outside the traditional mainstream, including interfaith families. A growing number of Reform Jews have begun to send their children to Reform and community-sponsored day schools, while summer camps and youth groups continue to attract large numbers of children from committed Reform families.

Approximately 26 percent of American Jews who are members of synagogues identify themselves as Conservative, making Conservative Judaism the second-largest Jewish movement in the United States. The movement's challenge is to find a way to attract more members to its synagogues, especially young people. A key strength is the Conservative Ramah camping movement and its network of Solomon Schechter day schools, which continue to graduate highly committed and Jewishly educated youngsters. These are the people who will determine the movement's future.

Reconstructionism is the mainstream Jewish movement with the smallest number of members. It remains an attractive choice for those seeking a worship experience that emphasizes intellectual exploration and a democratic approach to synagogue organization and decision making. The Reconstructionist philosophy of Jewish decision making is that halachah (Jewish law) can strongly influence but should

The Ḥavurah and Jewish Renewal Movements

In the early 1960's some Reconstructionist Jews began to come together in small, informal gatherings, or ḥavurot, to pray and engage in religious study and discussions. By the late 1960's and early 1970's Jewish social activists developed an increased interest in Jewish religious observance and helped start their own ḥavurot in Washington, D.C., Boston, New York, Los Angeles, and other communities. The ḥavurot held weekly Shabbat services and sponsored cultural activities.

Combining the idealism, individualism, and informality of 1960's culture with traditional Judaism, the ḥavurot attracted young Jews who rejected what they saw as the materialistic and impersonal aspects of the suburban world in which they were raised. Most ḥavurot prayer services were led by group members rather than by rabbis or cantors, and there was great openness to personalizing the prayer experience.

In recent years, the growing interest in spirituality has led to the growth of the Jewish Renewal movement. Its guiding force, Rabbi Zalman Schachter-Shalomi, has encouraged followers to enrich and deepen their spiritual lives through song, dance, prayer, and meditation. Some believe that Jewish Renewal may become a fifth movement within Judaism. For now, its greatest impact may be on the Reconstructionist, Reform, and Conservative movements. Many synagogues, for example, have integrated into their prayer services the songs and creativity that are characteristic of Jewish Renewal.

not fully determine decisions. This approach has helped encourage ritual experimentation and reaching out to interfaith families.

Looking to the Future

The American Jewish community has continually met the challenge of changing conditions and opportunities by adapting in diverse and creative ways. In our time, Judaism has been enriched by the Jewish feminist movement, social activism, and the creative innovations of communal and personal religious rituals.

Artist Mae Rockland Tupa's Ḥanukkah menorah is a tribute to her American and Jewish identities *and* to her sense of humor and creativity.

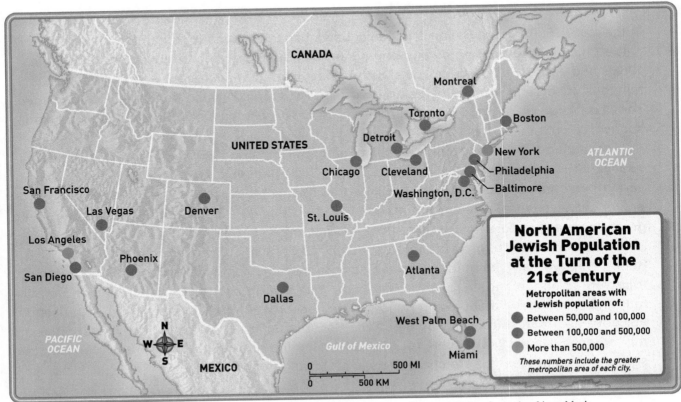

As of 2001, the three largest Jewish population centers in North America were—by far—the New York metropolitan area (2,051,000), Greater Los Angeles (668,000), and southern Florida (498,000).

Today, it is not unusual for bar and bat mitzvah ceremonies to be conducted for adults who did not have them when they were younger, many couples include personalized rituals in their Jewish wedding ceremonies, and some families now weave their own life experiences with the retelling of the Passover story at the seder. In addition, many American Jews strongly support Israel and are influential in matters of American and world politics, and synagogue adult and family education programs are evermore popular.

Yet there are still challenges. Increased rates of intermarriage and total assimilation, decreased birthrates among Jews, and decreased rates of conversion of non-Jews to Judaism cause some people to wonder whether Judaism will continue to thrive. Indeed, the American Jewish population is becoming an ever-smaller percentage of the American population.

The commitment to Jewish peoplehood—the traditional idea that all Jews, wherever they live, are related to one another and responsible for one another—has declined as assimilation

This portrait of bat mitzvah celebrant Eden Fried and her brothers, sisters, and cousins is a reminder that the Jewish future will be written by you and your generation, in all your diversity and through your many actions.

and intermarriage rise. A survey in 1998 found that only 52 percent of American Jews agreed with the statement, "I look at the entire Jewish community as my extended family," and only 47 percent agreed that "I have a special responsibility to take care of Jews in need around the world."

The modern Jewish community of North America brings enormous resources to help meet these challenges. Its members are diversely talented, holding positions of accomplishment in business, government, education, the arts, and sciences—in fact, throughout society. It has achieved much and surely will achieve more.

But despite our many resources, questions still remain. For example, which innovations in Jewish practice will be accepted into Jewish tradition? What levels and styles of participation in Jewish communal life will become most common? How will the ties among the various communities of the Diaspora be strengthened and challenged, and what relationship will Diaspora Jews have with the Jews of Israel?

The answers are not for this book to tell, for they are not yet known. You will learn them day by day as you and your generation both watch them unfold and make them happen.

May you go from strength to strength.

Glossary

A

Aliyah (Going up) Making *aliyah* refers to immigrating to and settling in the Land of Israel; an *aliyah* during a prayer service is the honor of going up to the *bimah* to recite the blessing over the Torah.

Allied Powers The countries who joined forces with the United States in World War I (Russia, France, and Great Britain) and in World War II (Great Britain and the Soviet Union).

Antisemitism Prejudice against Jews.

Apartheid Laws Laws of South Africa designed to keep people of different races from mixing.

Ashkenazic Jews Jews whose families originated in Germany.

Axis Powers During World War II, the joint forces of Nazi Germany, Italy, and Japan.

B

Babi Yar Site in the Ukraine where, over the course of two days, thirty-three thousand Jews were machine-gunned to death by the Nazis in 1941.

Balfour Declaration Official statement of the British government, issued on November 2, 1917, expressing its support of a national home in Palestine for the Jewish people.

Beta Israel (The House of Israel) Name by which Ethiopian Jews refer to their community.

Blacklists Lists of people in the United States who were suspected of having Communist ties during the McCarthy era. People whose names appeared on blacklists often could not find employment and were socially rejected.

Bolsheviks Radical Russian Communists who, under the leadership of Lenin, seized control of Russia in 1917.

C

Central Powers The nations led by Germany, Austria-Hungary, and the Ottoman Empire, that joined forces during World War I.

Communists People who believe in a social, economic, and political system that seeks to eliminate all private property in favor of a more equal distribution of resources among the population.

Concentration Camp Prison established for those who were considered enemies of the Nazis.

D

Diaspora Places Jews live outside of the Land of Israel.

Dictator A person who holds absolute power over a government and its people.

Displaced Persons People who were removed from their native country as a result of World War II. Also known as DPs.

DP Camps Temporary facilities, refuge camps, for displaced persons.

E

Egalitarian Whereby men and women are treated with equality.

Eidot Hamizraḥ Jews from Middle Eastern and North African countries. Also called Mizraḥi Jews.

Ellis Island Leading federal immigration station in the United States from 1892 to 1954.

Emancipation Political freedom that enabled Jews to become full-fledged citizens of their countries with all the rights of other citizens.

Extermination Camp Concentration camp that was set up as a factory of mass murder.

F

Final Solution Hitler's plan to murder all of Europe's Jews.

G

The Great Depression The severe economic downturn that North America, Europe, and other industrialized areas of the world experienced in the 1930's. It caused many hardships including unemployment and poverty.

H

Haganah (Defense) Militia formed in 1920 to protect the Zionist community in Palestine.

Ḥalutzim (Frontline Soldiers or Pioneers) Jewish immigrants who came to Palestine shortly after World War I. The *ḥalutzim* were committed to "Hebrew labor," the Hebrew language, self-defense, and social justice.

Hamas An Islamic resistance movement that gained the support of many Palestinians in 2006 through its promise to end political corruption and to provide improved social services. It also was committed to the destruction of Israel.

Hatikvah (The Hope) Originally, the hymn of the Zionist movement, Hatikvah is Israel's national anthem.

Havurah Movement An organized effort that began in the early 1960's, the movement encourages the establishment of small, informal gatherings of Jews for the purpose of prayer, celebration, religious study, and participation in social action programs.

Hezbollah (Party of God) An Islamic political party and militant organization based in Lebanon that received military training and financial support from Iran.

Holocaust *(Shoah)* Hitler's deadly international campaign against the Jews. The Hebrew word for the Holocaust is *Shoah*.

I

Intifada (Shaking Off) Palestinian uprising against Israel that began in December 1987 in the West Bank and Gaza.

Irgun (Full name: *Irgun Tz'vei Leumi,* or National Military Organization) Formed in 1931, the Irgun operated in Palestine as an underground Jewish militia until 1948. It primarily was concerned with repelling Arab riots in Palestine and resisting Arab aggression.

Israel Defense Forces Name of Israel's military forces comprising the army, air force, and navy.

J

Jewish National Fund Organization created in 1901 to buy and develop land in Palestine for Jewish settlement. The land was to be jointly owned by the entire Jewish people.

Jews of Silence Term coined by Elie Wiesel to describe the oppressed Russian Jews.

K

Kibbutzim Villages created by *ḥalutzim,* or Jewish immigrants who settled in Palestine after World War I. These pioneers lived and worked together, owned all property jointly, and kept their money in a common treasury.

Knesset Israel's legislature.

Kristallnacht (Night of Shattered Glass) Government-supported pogrom against Jews throughout Germany on November 9, 1938.

L

Labor Movement The organized effort to improve working conditions. Workers formed unions to campaign in their own interest for better treatment from their employers. Jews have played leading roles in the labor movement.

Law of Return Israel's law that grants automatic citizenship to the families of all immigrants with a Jewish grandparent.

M

McCarthyism Aggressive style of accusing witnesses of Communist sympathies, usually without evidence. Intense anti-Communist suspicions persisted in the United States from the late 1940's into the 1950's.

Mein Kampf (My Struggle) Hitler's autobiography in which he spelled out his plan to seize power and rid Germany of its Jews.

Mizraḥi Jew *See* Eidot Hamizraḥ.

N

Nationalism Pride in one's country.

Nazi Party   The National Socialist German Workers Party, led by Adolf Hitler, which believed in the racial purity of the German people and saw Jews as a great enemy of Germany.

Nuremberg Laws   Enacted on September 15, 1935, laws that officially stripped German Jews of their basic rights, including German citizenship.

O

Operation Ezra and Nehemiah   The evacuation of 110,000 Jews from Iraq to Israel between 1950 and 1952.

Operation Magic Carpet   An airlift of about forty-seven thousand Jews from Yemen to Israel in 1949.

Operation Moses   A 1984 Israeli military operation in which thousands of Ethiopian Jews were brought to Israel.

Operation Solomon   A 1991 Israeli military operation in which thousands of Ethiopian Jews were brought to Israel.

P

Pale of Settlement   The land that is included in much of present-day Lithuania, Poland, Belarus, Ukraine, and Moldova. During the reigns of several czars, Jews were forced to live in this area.

Palestine   The name for the Land of Israel before it became the State of Israel in 1948.

Palestine Liberation Organization (PLO)   Palestinian resistance group founded in 1964.

Pogroms   Antisemitic riots and massacres.

Q

Quotas   Limits placed on the number of people—often from minority groups—who may join, work at, or attend an organization or institution, such as a university.

R

Righteous Gentiles   Non-Jews who risked their lives to save Jews during the Holocaust.

S

Sabras   Israeli-born Jews.

Sephardic Jews   Jews whose families originated in Spain or Portugal.

Shoah   See Holocaust.

Socialism   Economic, political, and social belief system that society should be based on cooperation rather than competition.

Sweatshops   Workshops or factories in which people work for long hours at low wages, and under unhealthy and unsafe conditions.

T

Tenement Houses   Buildings that meet minimum standards of safety, sanitation, and comfort, and are usually located in cities.

W

Warsaw Ghetto Uprising   The Jewish resistance against Nazi Germany's attempt to send the remaining Jews of the Warsaw Ghetto to concentration camps on the eve of Passover 1943.

Y

Yeshivas   Orthodox schools designed to carry on traditional Jewish learning and values.

Yishuv (Settlement)   Term for the Jewish community of Palestine before the establishment of the State of Israel in 1948.

Youth Aliyah   A project directed by Hadassah founder Henrietta Szold to help young Jews escape from Germany and settle in Palestine.

Z

Zionism   Movement to establish and support a modern Jewish state in the Land of Israel.

Index

A

Abdullah, King, 85
AFL. *See* American Federation of Labor.
Ahad Ha'am. *See* Ginsberg, Asher.
AIPAC. *See* American Israel Public Affairs Committee.
Alexander II, 2, 3, 4
Alexander III, 2, 3
Al-Husseini, Grand Mufti Haj Amin, 58, 59
aliyah, 20, 22 (def.), 83, 132. *See also* First Aliyah, Fourth Aliyah, Second Aliyah, Third Aliyah, Youth Aliyah.
Alliance Israélite Universelle, 103, 104
Allied Powers (World War I), 30, 31 (def.), 36, 132
Allied Powers (World War II), 70, 72 (def.), 73, 77, 78, 81, 132
American Federation of Labor (AFL), 14
American Israel Public Affairs Committee (AIPAC), 122, 124 (def.)
American Jewish Joint Distribution Committee (JDC), 30, 33 (def.), 34, 38, 39, 81, 87, 104
Amir, Yigal, 117
antisemitism, 2, 3–5, 22, 23, 24, 27, 28, 29, 30, 34, 35, 41, 45–47, 62, 65, 68, 69, 73, 81, 92, 93, 94, 95, 98, 100–102, 107, 112, 120, 132, 134. *See also* Jews, oppression of; Nazi Party.
apartheid laws, 100, 105, (def.), 106, 107, 132
Arab Revolt. *See* Great Uprising.
Arafat, Yasir, 116, 117, 118, 121
Ashkenazic Jews, 20, 21 (def.), 107, 132
Auschwitz, 75, 76, 83
Axis Powers, 70, 72 (def.), 132

B

Babi Yar, 70, 72 (def.), 132
Balfour Declaration, 30, 36 (def.), 52, 54, 57, 59, 73, 83, 132
Baline, Israel. *See* Berlin, Irving.
Bar Kochba Revolt, 32
Beckmann, Max, 63

Begin, Menahem, 60, 82, 117
Benderly, Samson, 48
Ben-Gurion, David, 26, 58, 59, 60, 84, 85, 86
ben Zvi, Yitzhak, 26
Berlin, Irving, 43, 47
Beta Israel (House of Israel), 110, 112 (def.), 132
Bialik, Hayyim Nahman, 8
blacklists, 90, 94 (def.), 132
Bloc of the Faithful. *See* Gush Emunim.
Bogen, Boris, 62
Bolsheviks, 30, 34 (def.), 132
Brandeis, Louis D., 31, 35, 36
Bub, Zelig, 105
Bund (General Jewish Works Union), 2, 3, 7 (def.), 8

C

Cahan, Abraham, 10, 11, 13, 18
Cardin, Shoshanah, 123, 126
Central Powers, 30, 31 (def.), 132
civil rights, 90, 91, 95, 96, 97–98, 102, 125
Clinton, Bill, 117
Communists, 30, 34 (def.), 46, 65, 66, 67, 72, 93–95, 107, 132, 133
concentration camp, 62, 68 (def.), 71, 72, 73, 74, 76, 80, 81, 132
Conference of Presidents of Major Jewish Organizations, 123, 126
Council of Jewish Federations, 126
crypto-Jews, 107

D

Dachau, 68, 80
death camps. *See* extermination camps.
Declaration of Independence, 85, 86
Depression. *See* Great Depression.
Diaspora, 20, 21 (def.), 25, 26, 29, 30, 34, 49, 52, 54, 80, 100, 105, 110, 115, 131, 132
dictator, 62, 68 (def.), 132
displaced persons (DPs), 80, 81 (def.), 82, 87, 132
DP camps, 80, 81 (def.), 82, 83, 132
DPs. *See* displaced persons.
Dreyfus, Alfred, 20, 23, 24

E

East Jerusalem. *See* Old City.
egalitarian, 122, 127 (def.), 128, 132
Egypt, vi, 84, 103, 110, 114, 117
Eichmann, Adolf, 123, 124
Eidot Hamizrah (Mizrahi Jews), 80, 87 (def.), 88, 103, 104, 111, 132
Eilberg, Amy, 127
Einstein, Albert, 62, 63, 64
Eisenstein, Judith Kaplan, 41–42
Ellis Island, 10, 13 (def.), 132
Elqānyān, Habib, 105
emancipation, vi, 9, 21, 23, 27, 29, 63, 132
Enlightenment. *See* Haskalah.
Eretz Yisrael. See Land of Israel.
"Ethics of the Sages." *See Pirkei Avot.*
Exodus 1947, 80, 83 (def.)
extermination camps, 70, 75 (def.), 76, 77, 78, 132

F

Fackenheim, Emil, 97
feminism, 120, 127–28
final solution, 70, 75 (def.), 132
First Aliyah, 20, 22 (def.)
First Temple, 20
First Zionist Congress, 20, 23 (def.), 24
Ford, Henry, 41, 46
Fourth Aliyah, 52, 53, 57 (def.)
Frank, Anne, 74
Frankfurt Free Jewish Lehrhaus, 62, 69
Freud, Sigmund, 63

G

Gaza Strip, 58, 84, 110, 111, 114, 117, 119, 134
General Jewish Workers Union. *See* Bund.
Gershwin, George, 43
Ginsberg, Asher, 25, 26
Golan Heights, 114, 116
Golden Decades, 90
Goldstein, Herbert, 51
Gompers, Samuel, 14
Goodman, Andrew, 97
Gordon, Aaron David, 26–27, 29
Goren, General Rabbi Shlomo, 115

Great Depression, 40, 41, 50 (def.),
67, 95, 133
Great Uprising, 53, 57–58, 60
Green, Shawn, 99
Greenberg, Hank, 90, 92, 99
Gush Emunim (Bloc of the Faithful),
110, 116 (def.), 133

H

Habad-Lubavitch, 102
Hadar Hacarmel, 55
Hadassah (Women's Zionist
Organization of America), 52,
56, 57, 84, 134
Haganah, 52, 54 (def.), 55, 57, 60,
80, 82, 83, 84, 133
Haifa, 55, 57, 83, 84, 100
halutzim, 52, 55 (def.), 133
Hamas, 110, 111, 119 (def.), 133
Hanukkah, 48, 52, 79, 99
Hashomer, 54
Haskalah (Jewish Enightenment),
3, 63
Hatikvah, 20, 23 (def.), 133
Havurah movement, 122, 129 (def.),
133
Hebrew, 8, 18, 22, 23, 28, 47, 48, 55,
58, 66, 69, 82, 85, 87, 103, 104,
114, 133
Hebrew University, 52, 55 (def.)
Herzl, Theodor, 20, 22–23, 24, 29,
84, 120
Heschel, Abraham Joshua, 96, 97
Hezbollah, 110, 119 (def.), 120, 133
High Holidays, 47, 98, 99
Hitler, Adolf, 46, 50, 56, 57, 59, 62,
63, 67–68, 70–73, 75, 77, 79, 90,
94, 97, 103, 107, 133, 134
Holocaust *(Shoah)*, 70, 71 (def.),
72–79, 81, 82, 87, 97, 100, 102,
120, 122, 123–24, 133, 134
Holocaust Remembrance Day *(Yom
Hashoah)*, 122, 123 (def.)
House of Israel. *See* Beta Israel.
Hovevei Tzion (Lovers of Zion),
20, 22 (def.)

I

IDF. *See* Israel Defense Forces.
Inquisition, 107
Intifada, 110, 116, 133
Iran, 101, 104–5, 120, 133
Iraq, 84, 87, 103, 134

Irgun, 52, 60 (def.), 80, 82, 84, 133
Israel Defense Forces (IDF), 110,
113 (def.), 117, 133
Israeli-Arab conflict, 52–54,
57–60, 80, 84, 85–86, 87–88,
103, 114–21, 124
Israeli Arabs, 86–88

J

Jabotinsky, Ze'ev (Vladimir), 32,
54, 60
JDC. *See* American Jewish Joint
Distribution Committee.
Jerusalem, 20, 21, 52, 54, 55, 59, 80,
82, 83, 84, 100, 103, 110, 114, 117
Jewish Brigade Group, 73, 81
Jewish Community Center (Buenos
Aires), 101, 107
Jewish Enlightenment. *See Haskalah.*
Jewish identity, 9, 10, 19, 20, 39, 40,
42, 46–47, 49, 52, 62, 69, 80, 90,
97, 100, 112, 128, 129
Jewish Legion, 31, 32
Jewish National Fund (JNF), 20, 21,
27 (def.), 57, 126, 133
"Jewish problem," 66–67, 70
Jewish Renewal movement, 122,
129 (def.)
Jewish Theological Seminary (JTS),
10, 18, 41, 48
Jewish unity, 80
Jews
American, 38, 40–51, 90–99,
122–31
Ashkenazic, 20, 21 (def.), 107
immigration to Palestine, 5, 8, 20,
21, 22, 25–28, 52, 53, 55, 57, 68,
71, 78, 82–83, 87–88, 103, 111–12,
132, 133
immigration to U.S., 5, 8, 9,
10–19, 28, 40, 50, 103
oppression of, 2, 3, 4–9, 18, 62–69,
101–3, 105, 106, 107. *See also* antisemitism.
refugees, 32, 50, 73, 75, 78, 80–81,
82–83. *See also* displaced persons.
in Russia, 3–9, 10–13, 17, 18, 25,
27, 31–32, 34, 37, 65
Sephardic, 10, 18 (def.), 21, 75,
107, 134
in Soviet Union, 101–3, 112
Jews for Urban Justice, 125
Jews of Silence, 100, 102 (def.), 133

JNF. *See* Jewish National Fund.
Jordan, 84, 85, 87, 111, 114, 117
JTS. *See* Jewish Theological Seminary.
Judaism
adaptation of, 3, 7, 19, 40, 42–44,
47–51, 62, 66–67, 97, 104, 121–31
Conservative, 43, 48, 49, 50, 95,
96, 98, 127, 128, 129
Orthodox, 33, 43, 47, 50, 62, 65,
66, 96, 112, 113, 122, 124, 127–28
prophetic, 90, 95 (def.), 98
Reform, 33, 41, 43, 47, 50, 63, 90,
95, 96, 97, 98, 127, 128
Jungreis, Esther, 122

K

Kaplan, Rabbi Mordecai, 41,
48–50, 51
Khrushchev, Nikita, 102
kibbutzim, 52, 55 (def.), 85,
113–14, 133
King, Martin Luther, Jr., 96
Knesset, 110, 113 (def.), 117, 133
Kook, Rabbi Zvi Yehudah, 116
kosher, 12, 19, 33, 44, 98, 113, 128
Koufax, Sandy, 99
Kristallnacht, 70, 71 (def.), 133
Ku Klux Klan, 91, 97

L

labor movement, 10, 14 (def.), 133
Land of Israel *(Eretz Yisrael)*, 7, 9, 17,
20–29, 30, 35, 38, 49, 66, 78, 84,
132, 134
Law of Return, 110, 112 (def.), 133
Lebanon, 119, 133
Lehi. *See* Lohamei Heirut Israel.
Lemlich, Clara, 11, 14
Lenin, Vladimir Ilich, 34, 132
Levitt, William, 90, 91
Liaison Bureau, 102
Lohamei Heirut Israel (Lehi), 82, 84
Lovers of Zion. *See Hovevei Tzion.*

M

ma'abarot, 80, 88 (def.)
mandate, 52, 53 (def.), 54, 57, 83
Mandela, Nelson, 105, 106
Marcus, David "Mickey," 80
Maskilim, 7
McCarthyism, 90, 93, 94 (def.), 95,
132, 133
McCarthy, Joseph, 94
Mein Kampf, 62, 68 (def.), 133

Meir, Golda, 83, 85, 100, 102
Messiah, 20, 22, 23, 66, 116
Mizrahi Jews. *See* Eidot Hamizrah.
Morais, Rabbi Sabato, 10, 18
Moses, 48
Myerson, Bess, 93
Myerson, Golda. *See* Meir, Golda.

N

Naqba, 86
Nasser, Gamal Abdel, 114, 124
National Council on Jewish
    Education, 41
nationalism, 20, 22 (def.), 36–37, 54,
    57, 66, 103, 134
Nationalist Socialist German Workers
    Party. *See* Nazi Party.
Nazi Party, 59, 62, 67 (def.), 68, 70,
    71–72, 73–76, 92, 96, 97, 107,
    132, 134
New City (West Jerusalem), 52,
    55 (def.), 115
Nicholas II, 4
Nuremberg Laws, 62, 63,
    68 (def.), 134

O

Old City (East Jerusalem), 52,
    55 (def.), 84, 114, 115
Operation Ezra and Nehemiah, 80,
    87 (def.), 134
Operation Magic Carpet, 80, 81,
    87 (def.), 88, 134
Operation Moses, 101, 109, 110,
    111 (def.), 134
Operation Solomon, 110,
    111 (def.), 134
Ottoman Empire, 18, 31, 36, 53,
    107, 132

P

Pahlavi, Mohammad Reza Shah, 104
Pale of Settlement, 2, 3 (def.), 4, 5, 8,
    134
Palestine, 2, 7 (def.), 8, 21, 23, 31, 32,
    36, 38, 41, 47, 49, 50, 52–61, 71, 73,
    80, 82–83, 85, 132, 133, 134. *See
    also* Land of Israel, State of Israel.
    Jewish migration to, 5, 8, 20, 21,
    22, 25–28, 52, 53, 55, 57, 68, 71,
    78, 82–83, 87–88, 103, 111–12
Palestine Liberation Organization
    (PLO), 110, 116 (def.), 117, 119,
    134

Palestinian Arabs, 26, 52–54, 57–60,
    83, 84, 110, 113, 116–21, 133
Palestinian refugees, 86, 87, 88
partition plan, 52, 58 (def.), 83, 103
Passover, vi, 20, 29, 33, 44, 113, 125,
    130, 134
Peel Commission, 58, 59
Peres, Shimon, 118
Pinsker, Leon, 22
Pirkei Avot ("Ethics of the Sages"), 66
PLO. *See* Palestine Liberation
    Organization.
pogroms, 2, 4 (def.), 5, 7, 8, 11, 12,
    17, 25, 27, 30, 34, 71, 78, 134
Priesand, Sally, 122, 127
Progressive Party, 100, 106
prophetic Judaism, 90, 95 (def.), 98
The Protocols of the Elders of Zion, 2, 3,
    4 (def.), 46, 120

Q

quotas, 40, 46 (def.), 47, 50, 59, 73,
    91, 134

R

rabbi, 95, 96, 97, 98, 104, 112, 122,
    124, 127, 128, 129
Rabinovitz, Solomon. *See* Sholom
    Aleichem.
Rabin, Yitzhak, 117, 118, 121
Reconstructionism, 40, 50 (def.),
    127, 128, 129
Reconstructionist Rabbinical
    College, 50
refugee camps. *See* DP camps.
Reichstag, 62, 68 (def.)
Righteous Gentiles, 70, 75 (def.), 134
Rishon L'tziyon, 22, 23
Roosevelt, Franklin, 42, 50
Rosenberg, Ethel, 90, 94
Rosenberg, Julius, 90, 94
Rosenzweig, Franz, 62, 69
Rosh Hashanah, 13, 99, 102, 113
Rothschild, Jacob, 97

S

sabras, 110, 111 (def.), 134
Sadat, Anwar, 117
Sarnoff, David, 43
Sasso, Sandy, 127
Schachter-Shalomi, Rabbi Zalman,
    129
Schneiderman, Rose, 42
Schwarz, Ann, 71

Schwerner, Michael, 97
Second Aliyah, 20, 21, 25 (def.),
    26–28, 55
Second Intifada, 110, 111, 117 (def.)
Second Temple, 2, 20
Sephardic Jews, 10, 18 (def.), 21, 75,
    107, 134
Shabbat, 12, 15, 95, 97, 98, 113, 129
Shapira, Rabbi Meir, 69
Sharon, Ariel, 119
Shoah. See Holocaust.
Sholom Aleichem, 6, 8
shtetls, 15, 32
Sinai Peninsula, 114, 117, 119
Six-Day War, 103, 110, 114 (def.),
    115, 119, 124
Socialism, 2, 7 (def.), 9, 26, 33, 55, 66,
    67, 94, 113, 134
social justice, 7, 9, 55, 95, 96, 97–98,
    125, 127, 133
Society for the Advancement of
    Judaism, 41
Stalin, Joseph, 62, 65, 72, 94, 101–2
State of Israel, 20, 32, 61, 64, 80, 81,
    83–89, 100, 101, 102–5, 107, 109,
    110–21, 123, 124, 130, 134
Student Struggle for Soviety Jewry,
    102
Suzman, Helen, 100, 106
sweatshops, 10, 15 (def.), 134
synagogue, 51, 65, 68, 71, 79, 90, 91,
    95, 98, 99, 102, 107, 125, 127, 128,
    129, 130
Syria, 84, 103, 114, 117, 119
Szold, Henrietta, 52, 56, 134

T

Technion, 52, 55 (def.)
Tel Aviv, 21, 27, 28, 55, 58, 84, 100,
    126
tenement houses, 10, 14 (def.), 134
Third Aliyah, 52, 55 (def.)
tikun olam, 125. *See also* social justice.
Torah, 44, 47, 48, 66, 127, 128, 132
Trumpeldor, Joseph, 30, 32, 54, 55
tzedakah, 17, 99, 124

U

Uganda Plan, 20, 23 (def.), 25
UN. *See* United Nations.
United Jewish Appeal, 68
United Nations (UN), 81, 82, 103,
    116

United Nations Relief and Rehabilitation Administration (UNNRA), 81

United Nations Special Committee on Palestine (UNSCOP), 82, 83

UNNRA. *See* United Nations Relief and Rehabilitation Administration.

UNSCOP. *See* United Nations Special Committee on Palestine.

U.S. Holocaust Memorial Museum, 123, 124

W

Wald, Lillian, 10, 16

Wallenberg, Raoul, 75

War of Independence, 80, 84, 85, 86

Warsaw Ghetto Uprising, 70, 71, 76 (def.), 134

Wasserstein, Bernard, 100

Weizman, Chaim, 36, 37, 58

West Bank, 58, 84, 110, 111, 114, 116, 117, 119, 133, 134

West Jerusalem. *See* New City.

White Paper, 52, 53, 59 (def.), 82

Wiesel, Elie, 102, 122, 123, 133

Women's Zionist Organization of America. *See* Hadassah.

World War I, 17, 18, 30–35, 36, 38, 44, 45, 55, 62, 65, 67, 68, 69, 132, 133

World War II, 50, 56, 59, 70, 71, 72–79, 91, 92, 94, 95, 98, 100, 101, 103, 105, 107, 108, 128, 132

World Zionist Organization (WZO), 20, 23 (def.)

WZO. *See* World Zionist Organization.

Y

Yeshiva College, 47

yeshivas, 40, 48 (def.), 57, 134

Yiddish, 6, 8, 15, 17, 18, 19, 43, 47, 50, 51, 65, 69, 92, 102, 107

yishuv, 20, 25 (def.), 28, 54, 55, 58, 59, 60, 73, 82, 83, 134

Yom Hashoah. See Holocaust Remembrance Day.

Yom Kippur, 99, 117

Yom Kippur War, 110, 117

Youth Aliyah, 52, 56 (def.), 134

Z

Zionism, 20, 22 (def.), 23–29, 30, 32, 35–36, 37, 38, 47, 48, 49, 50, 52, 56, 57, 58, 59, 62, 65, 66, 80, 83, 84, 85, 95, 105, 114, 116, 124, 133, 134

Zion Mule Corps, 31, 32

www.ingramcontent.com/pod-product-compliance
Lightning Source LLC
Jackson TN
JSHW052136131224
75386JS00039B/1288